WHAT TO
DO ABOUT
NUCLEAR WASTE

WHAT TO
DO ABOUT
NUCLEAR WASTE

BY TRICIA ANDRYSZEWSKI

THE MILLBROOK PRESS
BROOKFIELD, CONNECTICUT

Library of Congress Cataloging-in-Publication Data
Andryszewski, Tricia. 1956–
What to do about nuclear waste / by Tricia Andryszewski.
p. cm.
Includes bibliographical references and index.
Summary: an extensively documented and well-researched
examination of the problems caused by nuclear waste from
the nuclear power industry and nuclear weapons programs.
ISBN 1-56294-577-7 (lib. bdg.)
1. Radioactive waste disposal—Juvenile literature. 2. Nuclear
power plants—Environmental aspects—Juvenile literature.
3. Nuclear weapons plants—Environmental aspects—Juvenile
literature. [1. Radioactive waste disposal. 2. Radioactive
wastes—Environmental aspects. 3. Nuclear power plants.]
I. Title.
TD898.A62 1995 363.72'89—dc20 94-44662 CIP AC

Photos courtesy of Photo Researchers: pp. 10 (© Scott Camazine),
36 (© Earl Roberge/Science Source), 48 (© Mere Woods/Science
Source); AP/Wide World Photos: pp. 13, 25, 41; UPI/Bettmann: pp.
20,59, 67: New Jersey Newsphotos: p. 30; Photofest: p.33; Energy
Technology Visuals Collection, Department of Energy: pp. 43, 52,
84, 88, 95, 99, 114; Bettmann Archive: p. 71; The Liaison Network:
pp. 72 (© Gamma Moscou), 105 (© Kaku Kurita); Reuters/Bettmann:
pp. 75, 108. Illustration on p. 16 by Frank Senyk.

CONTENTS

WHAT TO
DO ABOUT
NUCLEAR WASTE

CHAPTER ONE
THE BOMB AND
NUCLEAR BASICS

During World War II, as United States scientists raced to develop and test the world's first *nuclear weapon*, some of those working on the top-secret project discussed an awful possibility. Exploding such a bomb might, they thought, trigger a chain reaction in the air itself, setting the world's atmosphere on fire and incinerating all life on the planet's surface. Physicists calculated that the chances of this happening were only three in one million. The project's directors decided that this was a reasonable risk to take.[1]

When the world's first nuclear explosion, code-named Trinity, lit up the New Mexico desert on July 16, 1945, it did not ignite the atmosphere. It did, however, spew bits of *plutonium* and other dangerous *radioactive* particles hundreds of miles around the test site. The explosion also left behind an inevitable by-product of nuclear weapons production: lots of hazardous waste.

Nuclear waste from Trinity, and from the production and explosion of the two bombs that weeks later

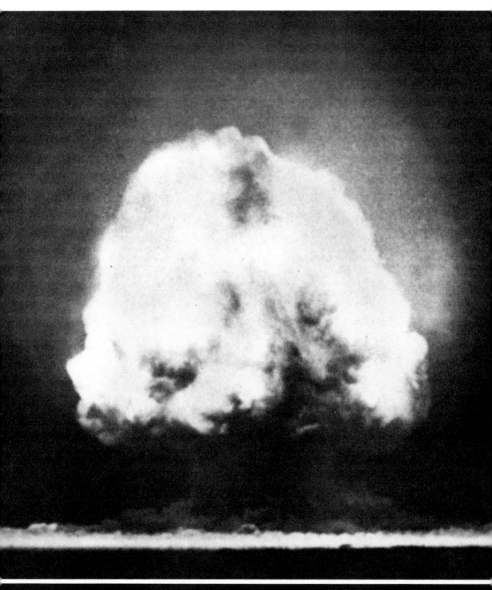

First atom bomb blast, July 16, 1945, New Mexico.

killed or maimed hundreds of thousands in Hiroshima and Nagasaki, Japan, remains dangerous today—and much of it will remain dangerous for thousands of years into the future. Over the past half century, nuclear weapons production, nuclear power, and other uses of nuclear technology have left the world with mountains of nuclear waste. What to do with it all is a daunting problem indeed.

NUCLEAR ARMS RACE

A sense of wartime urgency drove the scientists selected for the Manhattan Project, the secret program to create the world's first nuclear bomb. Right up to the spring of 1945, not long before the defeat of Nazi Germany, Americans working on the bomb feared that German scientists (who had been leaders in the field of nuclear physics before the war) might build one first.

After the war, the U.S. government seriously debated placing nuclear technology under international control to avert a new *arms race*, this one with the Soviet Union. But no agreement was reached on effective controls, and the great Cold War arms race began. In 1949 the Soviet Union exploded its first nuclear weapon, over Siberia. In 1952 the United States exploded a bomb vastly more powerful than anything exploded previously: the first *thermonuclear weapon*, the hydrogen bomb, or H-bomb. In 1955 the Soviet Union exploded a primitive thermonuclear bomb. Each country created an entire nuclear industry to build up stockpiles of nuclear weapons.

Like the Manhattan Project, the U.S. nuclear weapons buildup proceeded in great secrecy, with the government relying heavily on a few large contractors to handle the work. In 1961, President Dwight D. Eisenhower, a five-star general, warned the nation as he left office about the dangers of America's growing *military-industrial complex*, a powerful alliance of a few large corporations, large universities, and the military, with most of its activities kept hidden from the public. The Cold War nuclear and conventional weapons race created and funded the military-industrial complex. By the time Eisenhower left office, the United States had deployed or was still building 1,100 nuclear missiles.

Beginning in 1946 on remote islands in the South Pacific, and after 1951 in Nevada, the United States exploded hundreds of nuclear devices in test shots underground, underwater, and—in the early years—in the air, spewing radioactive waste directly into the atmosphere. These were not only tests of our weapons but also tests of our troops. The armed services deliberately exposed hundreds of thousands of military personnel and civilians to *fallout* from these tests—often at very close range—to learn how U.S. armed forces might function in a nuclear war.

TESTS ARE BANNED, BUT
THE ARMS RACE CONTINUES

By 1953, fallout was measurably raising levels of radioactivity thousand of miles from either U.S. or Soviet test sites. The U.S. government repeatedly reassured its

In September 1945 a U.S. soldier holds a green,
glasslike cinder—formed when the desert sand
crystallized in the intense heat of the blast.

citizens that fallout from the tests posed no danger. In the politically charged climate of the Cold War 1950s, critics of fallout were called Communist dupes. Nonetheless, public concern grew.

Public concern turned to public outcry in 1958, when high levels of *strontium 90* (a *radioisotope* released during the atmospheric tests) were found in baby teeth collected from American children. Fallout from nuclear testing had spread throughout the atmosphere around the world. Fallout had contaminated the rain with dangerous radioisotopes, which became part of the grass eaten by cows, and were passed on in the cows' milk to children. Mistaking the radioisotopes for calcium, the children's bodies concentrated them in their teeth and bones. The damage done by this contamination has developed slowly over decades. In 1991 a study commissioned by International Physicians for the Prevention of Nuclear War estimated that the fallout from atmospheric testing will eventually cause 2.4 million cancer deaths worldwide.[2]

In 1963 the United States, the Soviet Union, and Great Britain agreed to ban atmospheric nuclear tests. Underwater and underground testing continued. The United States conducted over one thousand underground nuclear tests before testing was suspended in 1990.[3] As of 1995, China was the only nation in the world still performing test explosions of nuclear weapons.

While testing continued, the arms race continued as well. Throughout the 1960s, 1970s, and 1980s, America's nuclear arsenal grew. In the process of manufacturing these weapons, the United States created a great deal of nuclear waste. In addition, civilian nuclear power has generated a large stream of nuclear waste that will continue to flow for many years to come.

To understand the effects of nuclear fallout, and why testing has been so controversial and nuclear wastes are so hazardous, requires some understanding of radiation and basic nuclear technology.

NUCLEAR BASICS

To make a nuclear weapon, technicians assemble a concentrated package of fissionable material. *Fissionable* means that the material's atoms can be broken apart, like certain isotopes of *uranium* and plutonium. When enough fissionable material is packed together, a *nuclear chain reaction* can occur. A neutron, one of the particles of which atoms are made, hits a fissionable atom, which then breaks apart, yielding two smaller atoms, a huge amount of energy, and two or more additional neutrons. These neutrons, in turn, strike other fissionable atoms, which then split apart and fuel the nuclear chain reaction.

In a bomb this happens very quickly. The energy released by millions of atoms splitting apart creates a devastating explosion. (In a thermonuclear weapon, or H-bomb, this *fission* reaction merely sets the stage for a vastly more powerful nuclear *fusion* reaction—the kind of reaction that powers the sun—fueled by certain isotopes of hydrogen.) In a nuclear power reactor, which uses the power of fission to supply electricity, technicians immobilize enough of the spare neutrons to slow down the nuclear chain reaction so they can control it

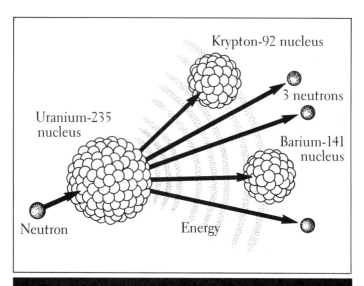

A neutron bombards the nucleus of a uranium-235 atom yielding an enormous amount of energy, two more atoms, and two or more neutrons. These neutrons can then bombard other nuclei causing a nuclear chain reaction.

and keep it going steadily. This prevents an explosion and makes it possible to harness the reaction's heat energy.

All of America's commercial nuclear power plants are fueled with fissionable uranium (U 235) derived from naturally occurring ore. Bombs are fueled with much higher concentrations of fissionable uranium and with plutonium. (Although nuclear technology uses other fissionable materials, these two are the most important.) Plutonium is actually manufactured in *nuclear reactors*. Inside a nuclear reactor, while the fissionable isotope uranium 235 fuels the chain reaction, *nonfis-*

sionable uranium 238 changes into plutonium 239. Processing uranium ore into fuel, "burning" it in a nuclear reactor, then *reprocessing* the spent fuel to separate and extract plutonium, is altogether very expensive. But plutonium makes a deadly powerful bomb, and weapon producers have been willing to pay dearly for it.

RADIATION

Part of the price paid for plutonium—and for other nuclear materials too—is radioactive nuclear waste. The nuclear fuel cycle generates hundreds of kinds of radioisotopes (unstable atoms that give off radiation while they decay into more stable structures). Some radioisotopes are more intensely radioactive than others, and some remain radioactive longer than others. Each radioisotope has a distinctive *half-life* (the length of time a sample of it takes to emit half of its radioactivity). Half-lives of radioisotopes range from a fraction of a second to millions of years. As a radioisotope decays, it may turn into yet another radioisotope (called a decay product), which will have its own distinctive half-life and intensity of radiation.

Each radioisotope emits a characteristic pattern of one or more of three types of radiation—alpha, beta, and gamma radiation. *Alpha radiation* can do the most severe localized damage to living tissue, but it is the least penetrating. It can't pass through human skin; even a piece of paper will stop it. But if a long-lived radioisotope that emits alpha radiation is inhaled or swallowed or gets into a wound, even a tiny speck can do terrible damage. The longer it remains embedded in living tissue, the more harm it's likely to cause. Alpha radiation is emitted by the decay products of some radioactive elements found in nature (uranium, thorium, and radium) and by long-lived *transuranics* (by-products of nuclear technology that are heavier than uranium) such as plutonium.

Beta radiation can penetrate skin but is most likely to damage people when it is ingested and the body mistakes it for a chemically similar element. For example, radioactive strontium is mistaken by the body for calcium, as mentioned earlier in this chapter. *Gamma radiation* has still greater penetrating power; it can even pass through wood. Most nuclear waste emits beta or gamma radiation, often both.

Radiation harms living creatures by damaging individual atoms inside individual cells. A massive dose of radiation can scramble enough cells so badly that the victim's body can no longer function, leading to death within a few painful weeks. With lesser doses, the damaged cells can survive to reproduce damaged copies of themselves. The cumulative impact of these radiation-affected cells multiplying, perhaps over many years, can create a variety of harmful health conditions, from thyroid problems to genetic disorders to cancers. Children and fetuses are especially vulnerable to harm from exposure to radiation. Because they are growing quickly, their cells multiply quickly. The effects of radiation keep multiplying too.

No one knows for sure how much radiation is a safe amount to receive. People exposed to high doses of radiation die, people exposed to lower doses get sick, and people exposed to still lower doses suffer no apparent ill effects. All of us are exposed to some radiation. A small amount of natural "background" radiation seeps from the earth and bombards us from space. We receive additional small doses from medical X rays (similar to but having much less energy than gamma radiation). It is often difficult to track or measure the long-range effects of radiation exposure. Cancers and other diseases caused by exposure to low levels of radiation can take years to show up, and these diseases can be caused by other factors. Increasingly, however, scientists suspect that no dose of radiation is low enough to be considered free of risk.

MINING, MILLING, AND PROCESSING

The nuclear fuel cycle for either power plants or weapons construction starts at a uranium mine, where raw uranium ore is dug out of the earth. Wastes produced at the mine include radon gas and radioactive dust.

The raw uranium ore is milled (processed) into *yellowcake*, a crude, yellow uranium oxide. Milling releases more radon and dust, as well as piles of mill tailings—fine-grained sand and dirt laced with very low concentrations of various radioisotopes, some of which have very long half-lives. Milling removes most of the uranium from the ore but leaves other radioisotopes and about 85 percent of the ore's radioactivity in the tailings.[4] Twenty-seven million tons of tailings sit in piles at closed uranium mills around the country, mostly in the West. They have leached radioactivity into soil and groundwater, and have been blown on the wind to places where people live and onto the land where livestock feed.[5]

A worker drills holes for explosive charges that will loosen uranium ore in a mine in New Mexico.

The chief health hazard associated with mill tailings, however, is *radon gas*, which can cause lung cancer. In open spaces, fresh air dilutes radon. In closed spaces, such as houses built on soil that gives off radon (as in New England, where much of the subsoil naturally gives off the gas), radon builds up to dangerous concentrations. In the 1960s, concrete made from mill tailings was used in buildings constructed in Grand Junction, Colorado, and several other western towns.

Many of the people living and working in these buildings were exposed to far higher levels of radon gas than are found even in uranium mines. The federal government has spent millions of dollars replacing the foundations of many of these buildings.[6]

The 1978 Uranium Mill Tailings Radiation Control Act made the Department of Energy (DOE) responsible for all of the tailings left at abandoned mines that used to supply the government with uranium. The act also required the DOE to clean up or stabilize other sites contaminated by tailings, such as the contaminated buildings in Colorado. Operators of active mines became responsible for their own mill tailings. (By 1992 most uranium used in the United States was imported, because imports had become so much cheaper; only one American mine remained active.)[7]

After mining and milling, the next step in the nuclear fuel cycle is processing—the conversion of yellowcake to *enriched* uranium fuel. In the United States, nuclear power reactors use fuel with a 3 to 4 percent concentration of uranium 235; nuclear weapons require a much greater concentration, called *highly enriched uranium*, or HEU. Processing generates small amounts of gas and liquid wastes, as well as larger amounts (although much less than the amount of tailings) of lightly radioactive solid wastes.

Pellets of enriched uranium fuel, packed into long, slim metal casings, make up the "fuel rods" used to run nuclear reactors. A set of fuel rods freshly installed in a reactor's core will keep a nuclear power reactor going for three to four years. During this time, fission fragments and other products of nuclear and chemical reactions accumulate in the fuel rods and begin to interfere with the nuclear chain reaction. When the chain reactions become too inefficient, the reactor is shut down and the spent fuel rods are removed and replaced with fresh fuel.

WASTES FROM
NUCLEAR POWER REACTORS

Civilian nuclear power reactors produce high-level and low-level radioactive wastes. *High-level waste* is the used reactor fuel; *low-level waste* is everything else, from discarded protective clothing to contaminated equipment. Low-level waste might emit any combination of alpha, beta, or gamma radiation, produced by radioisotopes with very short or very long half-lives. It is much less radioactive than high-level waste. Low-level nuclear waste produced in the United States has typically been buried in shallow landfills.

High-level wastes require much more careful handling than low-level wastes. "Spent" fuel hasn't lost its radioactivity; on the contrary, it is dangerously radioactive. Spent fuel direct from a nuclear reactor is bluish green and intensely hot and glows in the dark. If you go anywhere near it unshielded, you'll die from acute radiation poisoning.

Fortunately, most of the radioisotopes in high-level waste have relatively short half-lives. Within a few years, much of the waste's heat and radioactivity dissipates. Even so, high-level wastes emit still hazardous amounts of beta and gamma radiation for 500 to 1,000 years, and their alpha radiation remains a potent hazard for thousands of years.

Neither the United States nor any other nation has yet devised a satisfactory permanent method for disposing high-level nuclear wastes. The search for a solution to this problem has been both technically and politically difficult. At present, all the high-level nuclear waste ever produced in the United States remains in temporary storage.

NUCLEAR WASTES FROM WEAPONS PRODUCTION

To make America's nuclear weapons, government contractors for years "reprocessed" the spent fuel from nuclear reactors that were built specifically to create plutonium. Reprocessing, which chemically separates plutonium from the spent fuel, generates especially hard-to-handle high-level wastes mixed with various hazardous chemicals. Reprocessing also generates large quantities of low-level wastes. In recent years, the government has required that weapons facilities separate both mixed wastes (those contaminated with hazardous chemicals as well as radioisotopes) and long-lived transuranic wastes (produced by weapons plants in significant quantities) from low-level wastes. Mixed-waste disposal is governed by a complicated tangle of regulatory authority spread among the DOE, the Nuclear Regulatory Commission (NRC), the Environmental Protection Agency (EPA), and various state and local authorities. Transuranic wastes, like high-level wastes, sit in temporary storage awaiting implementation of a permanent disposal plan.

TRANSPORTING NUCLEAR WASTES

Sooner or later, large amounts of high-level and transuranic nuclear waste will need to be transported from weapons production facilities scattered all around the country to permanent or temporary waste repositories. Likewise, large amounts of waste generated by commercial power plants will require transport.

A traffic accident involving these nuclear materials could be catastrophic. Government regulators take two approaches to reducing the risk of such a catastrophe: rules to make sure that nuclear materials are safely packaged, and regulations to ensure that these materials are safely routed.

The packaging problem is fairly straightforward. U.S. Department of Transportation (DOT) and NRC regulations specify that nuclear materials, including nuclear waste, must be transported in a solid form (no radioactive liquids or gases) and must be enclosed in approved packaging designed to shield their radiation and to make sure that they are kept contained even in the case of an accident. The more dangerous the material, the more elaborate (and expensive) are the containers required for it.

The issue of the routes that shipments of nuclear wastes should be permitted to take and the precautions to be taken along these routes is more complicated, since local and state as well as federal regulators are involved. Most states have passed laws dealing with the transportation of nuclear waste; the DOT has challenged some of these laws in court, claiming that they conflict with federal regulations. Federal law does, how-

This 1982 photo shows technicians at the Indian Point nuclear power plant in Buchanan, New York, supervising the loading of low-level nuclear wastes for shipment to a dumping site.

ever, specify a role for the states. States must be notified before any high-level wastes can be shipped through them, and the DOE is required to provide funds for training state and local public-safety personnel to monitor shipments and to be ready for emergencies. Some states through which wastes might be transported en route to high-level and transuranic waste repositories (as of early 1995, approved sites had not yet been officially designated) have begun to set up inspection and emergency procedures.

The 1990 federal Hazardous Materials Transportation Uniform Safety Act directed the DOT to devise routing guidelines for all sorts of hazardous wastes, including all nuclear wastes. The federal effort to bring order to a chaotic patchwork of regulations will continue to evolve as storage and disposal sites for nuclear wastes are opened in the years to come.

CHAPTER TWO
NUCLEAR
POWER IN THE
UNITED STATES

As *we have seen,* America's earliest nuclear technology was dedicated to weaponry. After World War II, in 1946, Congress handed over the government's wartime nuclear apparatus to a new, civilian-run agency, the Atomic Energy Commission. The AEC became responsible for all aspects of nuclear weapons production, and for nuclear power development. In the early years, weaponry dominated.

The federal government, through the AEC, retained control not only of nuclear materials but also of nuclear research, even research on purely civilian applications. Furthermore, the AEC became responsible for both the promotion of nuclear technology and its regulation—that is, devising and enforcing rules to protect public health and safety and to govern waste disposal.

This conflict of interest, between promotion and regulation, together with the concentration of the new nuclear industry in the hands of relatively few people, and its continuing secrecy and tight security, all discouraged careful, objective consideration of the broader consequences of nuclear technology. One of these consequences has been the problem of nuclear waste, which in the early days of the nuclear age was handled far more carelessly than it is today. Cleaning up after that carelessness has added greatly to the costs of nuclear waste disposal.

During the 1950s, Congress loosened up on secrecy to encourage private companies to develop commercially viable nuclear plants, and to get ready to create and enter a new international market for nuclear power. The U.S. government retained control and even actual ownership of fissionable materials. U.S. corporations, sensing a potentially huge business opportunity, eagerly set to work on nuclear power.

The nuclear power business nearly died at birth, however—not because it couldn't meet its technical challenges but because it simply couldn't get insurance. A catastrophic nuclear reactor or nuclear waste disaster might be unlikely, but if it were to happen, its costs would be astronomical. No insurance company could underwrite such a risk; even if it could, no power company could afford to pay the insurance premium.

To get around the insurance problem, Congress offered power companies a unique solution. The Price-Anderson Act, passed in 1957 and renewed several times since, required utilities operating nuclear power plants to buy only a *limited* amount of liability insurance ($60 million at first, an amount commercial insurance companies could handle). The federal government would provide an additional limited amount of coverage ($500 million in 1957). Congress raised these ceilings several times over the years. If an accident were to occur at a nuclear power plant, private insurance would pay for any damages up to its limit, then the federal government would pay for any additional damages up to *its* limit. To pay for damages beyond these combined limits, Congress could vote funds to cover them—or not. (In a 1966 revision of the Price-Anderson Act, Congress did promise to take "whatever action is deemed necessary and appropriate to protect the public from the consequences" of a nuclear accident.)[1] The Price-Anderson Act freed nuclear power plants from financial responsibility for damages an accident might cause beyond specified limits.

Supported by this unprecedented indemnification, the nuclear power industry grew rapidly. Government and industry joined forces to build the first U.S. civilian nuclear reactor, the first in the world devoted exclusively to the generation of electricity, at Shippingport, Pennsylvania. (On line from 1957 to 1982, the Shippingport plant started as a public-relations coup for the "peaceful atom" but ended amid controversy about radioactivity released during its operation. As a source of electricity, the plant was never economically competitive with other sources, such as water, gas, or coal.)

The first nuclear power plant built solely for commercial purposes by commercial contractors was ordered for Oyster Creek, New Jersey, in 1963. It was offered to the utility company on a "turnkey contract" (the utility agreed to pay a flat fee for a fully built plant, with any cost overruns to be absorbed by the manufacturer) at a price that made it seem competitive with a natural-gas or coal-burning plant. Like several other early nuclear power plants, Oyster Creek was considered a loss leader.

The Oyster Creek, New Jersey, nuclear
power plant — the first nuclear power
plant built solely for commercial purposes
by commercial contractors.

(*Loss leader* is the term used to describe a barg
fered at a below-cost price to lure customers in
store in the hope that some of them will buy
profitable items.) If this was the nuclear industry's
egy, it worked. Within five years after the Oyster Creek
order, American utility companies had placed orders for
seventy-five nuclear power plants.[2]

After the go-ahead years of the 1960s, the nuclear
power industry ran into two formidable obstacles: public
resistance and unfavorable economics. Throughout the
1970s, concerned by accumulating reports of accidents
and damage done by military and civilian nuclear operations, growing numbers of activists fought the nuclear
power industry over safety issues. Beset by controversy,
the AEC was abolished in 1974. Congress assigned its
regulatory responsibilities to a new, independent
agency, the Nuclear Regulatory Commission (NRC);
the AEC's promotional functions were ultimately absorbed by the Department of Energy (DOE).

By this time, the glamour of the "peaceful atom"
was gone, and the economics of nuclear power were
looking more and more dismal. In the 1970s construction of all those nuclear power plants ordered in the late
1960s was taking longer than expected, just as interest
rates were rising. Costs escalated dramatically. Worse,
U.S. electric consumption didn't rise as much as expected in the 1970s. Many utility companies found
themselves able to generate more electricity than they
needed. Ordering an expensive nuclear reactor became
less and less attractive.

Then, in 1979, mistakes made by technicians at
the Three Mile Island nuclear power plant, in eastern
Pennsylvania, led to a near-total *meltdown* (destruction
of the reactor's radioactive core by an out-of-control nu-

clear reaction). Small amounts of radioactivity escaped from the plant; vast amounts of radioactive contamination remained inside the plant, awaiting a $1 billion cleanup.

Coincidentally, the movie *The China Syndrome* was released around the time of the Three Mile Island incident. This popular film presented the dramatic, though erroneous, notion that a meltdown in a nuclear power plant in North America might burn its way straight through the earth to China. Public fears about what could have happened at Three Mile Island were a public-relations disaster for the nuclear power industry.

No new nuclear power plants were ordered in the United States after the accident at Three Mile Island. Plants commissioned during the 1960s and 1970s have continued to operate, however, and they have continued to generate nuclear waste at each stage of the nuclear fuel cycle.

MOVEMENT AWAY
FROM NUCLEAR POWER

Beginning in 1993, the Clinton administration pursued an energy agenda wary of nuclear power. Existing nuclear power plants were to continue to operate, but future energy needs preferably were to be met by other means, such as natural gas, conservation, and renewable energy sources. In keeping with this agenda, the Clinton administration shifted funding away from nuclear power research and development. Between 1948 and 1992, fully 65 percent of the federal government's

The movie *The China Syndrome* was released around the time of the accident at Three Mile Island, fueling the public's fears about what could happen if a complete nuclear power plant meltdown occurred.

research-and-development funding for energy went to nuclear power.[3] By the end of George Bush's presidential administration, in 1992, funding had dropped slightly. The Clinton administration cut it further.[4]

It wasn't only the federal government that moved away from nuclear power in the United States. State and local governments as well as utility companies around the nation rethought the nuclear power equation. Given all of the technology's unanticipated costs, especially costs connected with nuclear waste, did it really make sense to operate nuclear power plants? As early as 1976, California's state legislature decreed that no new nuclear power plants should be built in the state until the federal government came up with a "demonstrated technology or means for the disposal of high-level nuclear waste." Seven other states soon passed similar legislation.[5] Individual utility companies, too, decided to shut down reactors ahead of schedule or to cancel construction of new reactors in order to save money.

More than one hundred nuclear power reactors operate or have operated at seventy-odd sites across the United States. Each reactor has been licensed to generate electricity for twenty-five to forty years, depending on its design. Although the NRC has considered extending at least some power plant licenses beyond forty years, many plants are expected to close well before the end of their original licensing periods. In 1991 the DOE estimated that 65 of the 109 reactors then operating would be shut down permanently by the year 2020.[6] The shut-down reactors won't be replaced by new reactors coming on line. By 1993 only one reactor (the Tennessee Valley Authority's Watts Bar project) remained under construction in the entire United States.[7]

SHUTTING DOWN
A NUCLEAR PLANT

Shut-down nuclear power plants are themselves a sort of nuclear waste. While the reactor is operating, during the nuclear fission process, the reactor's fuel and the structures surrounding it are bombarded by neutrons. As a result, some of the steel, water, and concrete surrounding the fuel rods become highly radioactive. In the same manner, as well as through the inevitable minor accidents that happen over the many years of plant operation, some of the plant structure becomes radioactive, though much less intensely than that which is near the reactor core. When the plant is decommissioned, all of this radioactivity must be contained and prepared for disposal. There are three internationally recognized ways of properly decommissioning a shut-down nuclear power plant:

1. *Immediate dismantlement.* The plant is dismantled as soon as it is shut down. All nuclear wastes are immediately sent to a disposal site, and the plant site itself is cleaned up and released for unrestricted use. This obviously appealing option runs up against two main obstacles: Handling a very hot, just-shut-down reactor presents formidable (and expensive) technical problems, and at present there's no place in the United States to send high-level wastes for disposal.

2. *Safe storage with later dismantlement.* The spent fuel is removed from the reactor, and contaminated areas are made secure for a specified period of time (10, 20, or 25 years would be appropriate), during

[35]

The Trojan nuclear power plant near Portland, Oregon, is one of the many nuclear plants that have been shut down or are expected to close permanently by 2020.

which much of the plant's radiation decays, leaving technicians with an easier site to clean up. The chief drawback of this approach is that it can cost up to $21 million per year to securely store and monitor nuclear wastes at a shut-down plant.[8] And, since it has never been done, no one knows how much easier or cheaper it might be to complete the cleanup later, after the wastes have cooled, rather than sooner.

3. *Entombment.* After all spent fuel and easily removable nuclear wastes are taken from the shut-down plant for disposal, the reactor is sealed inside steel or concrete, in which it remains long enough for its radioactivity to decay to a level at which no additional cleanup is needed. The problem with entombment is that decay to safe levels of radioactivity can take a very long time. The NRC decided to allow entombment only in cases where this decay would take less than 100 years. A few small, specialized research reactors pass this test; nuclear power reactors don't.

THE TIP OF THE ICEBERG

Although medicine, industry, and scientific research have all generated some nuclear waste, most of it has come from nuclear power plants and from weapons facilities. Plans for managing nuclear wastes are not yet set, and the waste we've seen so far is only the tip of the iceberg. As more and more weapons plants and nuclear power reactors come to the end of their useful lives, decommissioning and cleaning up the sites will generate still more waste.

How much cleanup the American people are willing to pay for will ultimately be decided in the political arena. The grandest goal would be to decontaminate nuclear sites thoroughly enough that they could be released for "unrestricted use"—clean enough to become building sites for homes or schools. This may not be technically feasible at some sites (especially at some military facilities), and at other sites it would be astronomically expensive.

Cleanup priorities will also be sorted out in the political arena. Which disposal facilities should be built first, and where they should be sited? Are permanent solutions within our grasp, or should we be concentrating on keeping nuclear wastes isolated and safe for the short term? Also, which contaminated sites should be cleaned up first: those presenting the most immediate dangers to human health or the environment, those that are easiest and cheapest to clean up quickly, or those that present the most typical problems, so that lessons can be learned for future cleanups?

CHAPTER THREE
CLEANING UP AFTER
NUCLEAR POWER

The dismantling of a nuclear power plant not only makes what to do with the spent fuel a more urgent concern but also generates a huge pile of low-level waste, more waste than was generated while the plant was running. With so many plants expected to be decommissioned in the future, a mountain of low-level waste lies ahead. At present we have no place to dispose of it.

LOW-LEVEL WASTE DISPOSAL

In the 1940s and 1950s most military and civilian nuclear wastes were buried in shallow graves on government property. (In addition, before 1970, the government packed some low-level waste into 55-gallon (208-liter) drums and dumped it at sea.) In the 1960s the government restricted its disposal sites to its own waste, mostly generated by the weapons program. Since siting and construction standards for these early waste disposal sites were less stringent than they are today, and since some of the waste buried at the sites is quite dangerous, several of the sites now threaten to harm public health or the environment and need to be cleaned up.

Since the 1960s civilian low-level wastes (mostly from nuclear power plants) have been put into landfills at sites chosen by state governments. Typically, the waste has been packed in containers, then the containers have been placed in large, shallow trenches. Filled trenches have been capped with clay or some other material that discourages rainwater from percolating through the trenches. Then the entire site has been graded to control drainage and erosion.

In 1980 the Low-Level Radioactive Waste Policy Act tightened standards for new low-level waste disposal sites. For political as well as technical reasons, it is unlikely that any such facilities opened in the future will use the old shallow-burial technology. People living nearby worry about the security and stability of the sites and about the possibility of groundwater contamination. Alternative technologies include placing the wastes in underground or aboveground vaults or in concrete bunkers mounded over with earth, or burying the wastes more deeply. These alternatives are more expensive than shallow burial in trenches.

The 1980 Act was Congress's response to an approaching low-level waste crisis. One by one, disposal sites around the country were closing. By the end of the 1970s only three remained open. The site at Barnwell, South Carolina, received 85 percent of the nation's

This photo taken in 1979 at the Hanford, Washington, site shows a pit containing low-level nuclear waste from Three Mile Island.

commercial low-level nuclear waste in the 1970s; in 1979, it announced plans to cut in half the amount it would accept. The nation's other two sites, in Nevada and Washington, also planned to institute restrictions.[1]

The 1980 legislation made each state responsible for finding some way to dispose of the waste generated within its borders. States were encouraged to form compacts with their neighbors and to plan and build regional sites that would share the burden of disposal fairly. By 1995, however, not a single new disposal site had been built. A sampling of the local and environmentalist opposition to specific sites and the political wrangling among the states demonstrates how this impasse developed:

• In 1992, voters in Boyd County, Nebraska, overwhelmingly rejected a proposal to construct a low-level disposal site in their county. The project would have received waste from Nebraska, Arkansas, Louisiana, Kansas, and Oklahoma.[2]

• In 1993, South Carolina threatened to cancel New York State's contract for dumping wastes at Barnwell, charging that New York wasn't serious about finding an alternative disposal site and emphasizing that residents of Barnwell wanted their site to close. In response, New York (which belongs to no regional compact) began to consider reopening a low-level disposal site at Ashford, New York, which had been closed in 1975 when water seeping into the landfill there overflowed.[3]

• Toward the end of 1993, citing unresolved environmental issues, the Clinton administration put on hold a transfer of federal land to California for a disposal site planned for Ward Valley, in the eastern Mohave

This 1989 photo shows transuranic waste packed
in 55-gallon (208-liter) steel drums at the
Savannah River site. Once all the space is used,
the slab is covered with earth.

Desert.[4] In 1994, as political pressures against the project mounted, a spokesman for the company that would run the project said: "From a national perspective, if we cannot put a disposal site here, you cannot put one anywhere."[5]

During the early 1980s, as waste disposal became more expensive and politically difficult, the overall volume of low-level nuclear waste being generated shrank somewhat, as hard-pressed waste producers became more careful about separating radioactive from nonradioactive materials. The overall amount of radioactivity remained about the same, concentrated in a smaller volume of waste. In the 1990s the key factor that determined the amount of low-level wastes being generated was the number of nuclear reactors being refueled each year. In the future, the key will be the number of plants being decommissioned.

Although the proportions varied from year to year, by the early 1990s about half of the volume (but most of the radioactivity) of civilian low-level nuclear wastes generated each year came from nuclear power plants. Perhaps another third of the volume came from industry, which used relatively small quantities of radioactive materials in enterprises ranging from biotechnology research to quality control operations. The rest, a comparatively small amount, came from a great many individual sources, including hospitals and clinics, and universities and other research centers.[6]

An unintended consequence of Congress's 1980 legislation was that by the early 1990s thousands of small users of radioactive materials had no place where they could afford to dispose of their low-level wastes.

The 1980 Act permitted the older disposal sites to refuse to accept waste from outside their regions after January 1, 1993, *whether or not new disposal sites were open by then*. No new sites opened up. By 1993 the Nevada site was closed and the Washington site was refusing to accept waste from outside its region, leaving only the Barnwell site to accept all the rest of the nation's nuclear wastes. Barnwell slapped a $220 per cubic foot (about 0.03 cubic meter) surcharge on all wastes from outside its region, declared that it would stop accepting *any* waste from outside its region in 1995, and announced that it would shut down altogether in 1996. Low-level nuclear wastes have piled up in thousands of sites around the country, as users with no place to go have improvised storage sites for their wastes.[7]

HIGH-LEVEL WASTE DISPOSAL

As frustrating and inconclusive as the low-level waste story has been, high-level nuclear wastes present greater problems. Although spent fuel from nuclear power plants accounts for only about 1 percent of the volume of all nuclear wastes, it contains about 95 percent of all the radioactivity of military and civilian wastes combined.[8] Obviously, it calls for very careful handling.

In the earliest days of nuclear power, government planners and power plant operators considered spent fuel to be a useful resource, not a waste disposal problem. Their assumption was that spent fuel would be chemically reprocessed to yield valuable uranium and plutonium. (Reprocessing also yields large amounts of nuclear waste, however, and no clear plans were made for handling it.) But the reprocessing of civilian spent fuel, as we shall explore in Chapter 6, turned out to be technically, politically, and economically unattractive, and it was abandoned in the United States.

As dozens of nuclear power plants came on line in the 1960s and 1970s, it became clear that the disposal of spent nuclear fuel was going to be a problem. The federal government began to look for a place to bury it. Its first choice, a deep salt deposit near Lyons, Kansas, was abandoned in the early 1970s because past drilling in the area for gas and oil had created a risk that groundwater might percolate through the site and become contaminated.

Other burial sites were investigated, but none were selected by the time Congress, in 1982, passed the Nuclear Waste Policy Act. This legislation directed the Department of Energy (DOE) to develop two deep burial sites for high-level nuclear wastes and implied that one should be located in the West and one in the East. The Nuclear Waste Policy Act set America firmly on the road to geologic burial of high-level wastes and turned the country away from exploring other options. It also set off years of political wrangling, since no state wanted to host such a permanent disposal facility. In 1987, Congress amended the legislation, abandoning the search for an eastern burial site and directing the DOE to focus on evaluating only one possibility: Yucca Mountain in Nevada.

The Nuclear Waste Policy Act also specified a way to pay for high-level waste disposal: the Nuclear Waste Fund. Nuclear power plants were required to pay a one-time fee into this fund to cover the disposal costs of all the high-level wastes they generated before 1983, plus a millage fee of 1 cent per kilowatt-hour for all electricity generated by nuclear power in the future.

In return for this money, Congress promised the utilities that the DOE would haul away their spent fuel for disposal by January 1998. The DOE would take title to the high-level waste as it left the power plant, and the costs of safely transporting and disposing the waste would be paid out of the Nuclear Waste Fund.

By the end of 1993, the DOE had spent about $3 billion from this fund (much of it in evaluating Yucca Mountain); about $4 billion remained in it, with more coming in from interest and from the millage fees.[9] Yet no disposal site had been officially named, and actual construction of a disposal facility seemed a long way off.

Meanwhile, spent fuel was piling up—tens of thousands of tons of it by the early 1990s. Almost all of it remained in temporary storage at the power plants where it was generated. Used fuel rods fresh from the reactor, intensely hot and radioactive, are stored at the plants in their metal cases on racks submerged in pools of water (called "swimming pools"). Pumps circulate the water in the pools, dissipating the heat thrown off by the cooling fuel.

Designers of nuclear power plants assumed that spent fuel would be stored on-site for only a short time (perhaps half a year to three years) while the fuel shed most of its heat and radioactivity. Then the partly cooled fuel would be shipped out of the plants for reprocessing or disposal. Instead, the swimming pools began to fill up. Most U.S. nuclear power plants have had

An example of used fuel rods being stored in "swimming pools." The spent fuel is still highly radioactive and continues to generate heat.

to rerack the spent fuel in their pools, packing the canisters as tightly as safety permitted to make room for as much fuel as possible.

By the early 1990s even the reracked pools were filling up. At least twenty-six plants are expected to run out of pool storage space by the year 2000.[10] Some power plants have begun to move partly cooled fuel to dry casks—heavily shielded containers that are stored aboveground and air-cooled rather than water-cooled.

Dry storage in a properly designed, well-shielded cask is not inherently dangerous. In fact, it has at least one clear safety advantage over water-cooled systems: Passive air cooling doesn't rely on mechanical pumps, which can break down. The Nuclear Regulatory Commission (NRC) asserts that spent fuel can be safely stored in dry casks for up to one hundred years, by which time the intensity of the radiation emitted by the spent fuel will have dropped by 90 percent or more.[11]

With nowhere else to put the waste, "we are sort of inching our way toward a policy of at-reactor storage," according to a former federal nuclear waste analyst.[12] But commercial nuclear reactor sites were selected with no more than 40 years of use in mind. To keep wastes at the plants indefinitely raises several issues. Are the sites technically and environmentally suitable for storage? (Many nuclear power plants are located beside rivers.) At what point are "temporary" fixes likely to fail? Will the communities that host these reactors tolerate a larger accumulation of high-level wastes at the plants, or wastes kept there for longer than originally planned? The last of these questions may prove to be politically decisive:

• The Palisades nuclear power station in Covert, Michigan, running out of room in its water-cooled storage, has been seeking permission to move some fuel into dry casks. Local activists have protested: How long will spent fuel be kept at the plant? Has anyone evaluated the plant site's appropriateness for long-term storage? Can the casks be maintained safely? Will they be? Is dry-cask storage a better option than simply retiring the plant when it runs out of pool space? [13]

• A nuclear power plant on the Mississippi River, near Minneapolis, will have to shut down in 1995 unless it gets permission to move some of its spent fuel into dry-cask storage. Pressured by local residents and environmentalists, the state legislature has balked at giving the plant permission. [14]

Shutting down plants early for lack of storage space, in addition to shutting down plants at the end of their planned life spans and for other reasons, could prove to be a very costly option for U.S. taxpayers. Shut-down plants don't generate electricity, and no electricity means no millage fees for the Nuclear Waste Fund. A 1993 congressional report expressed concern that the federal government might have to pick up much of the tab for high-level waste disposal:

> A possible source of future federal liability . . . would arise if the Nuclear Waste Fund proves inadequate to meet the program's costs. Such a development could result from continuing premature shutdowns of reactors and the lack of license renewals for existing

reactors, so that the fund has little income in the 2020 to 2040 time frame when costs for transportation and emplacement of wastes are expected to be high.[15]

The federal government clearly has a strong interest in opening up a permanent repository for high-level wastes as soon as possible. For many years, its best hope for such a repository has been Yucca Mountain.

YUCCA MOUNTAIN

By 1994, Nevada's governor, Bill Miller, knew that the odds were against him in his fight to stop the Yucca Mountain project:

> It's like a steamship that's going full bore, and they don't care if the dock is there or not. I mean, they don't know where else to go, so they're going to go right in, even if it's a dry dock. There's so much monetary investment [in the project so far], and it's such a simple political solution, since most of the waste is generated elsewhere, and it's easy to sell to constituents in other parts of the country that it should go in the desert.[16]

Nevadans have overwhelmingly opposed burying the nation's high-level nuclear waste at Yucca Mountain, but all parts of the state have not been equally opposed.

[51]

Controversy surrounds the proposed
plan to store high-level nuclear wastes
at Yucca Mountain, Nevada.

People living west of Yucca Mountain, nearer to the site and more likely to profit from business it might bring to the area, have been more likely to support it. People living to the east—and to the east of the Nevada Test Site as well—have been more suspicious of the project. Their homes lie downwind from the old nuclear weapons testing grounds, where higher concentrations of radioactive fallout fell during the atmospheric testing of the 1950s and 1960s.[17]

Colorado and Nebraska, states along the likely transport routes to Yucca Mountain, have also expressed concern about the site. Furthermore, the Western Shoshone Indians claim Yucca Mountain as sacred ground. It's Nevada, however, that the DOE has blamed for much of the delay in evaluating the site, a process that dragged on for two decades.[18] The DOE has lobbied Congress to reduce Nevada's role in the site review process.[19] DOE geologist Tom Bjerstedt has asserted: "If you can't site it in Nevada, our political process in our society is just too immature to have ever created this waste in the first place, because we don't know how to handle it."[20]

Geologists use several criteria to evaluate a site such as Yucca Mountain for possible use as a high-level waste repository. They're looking for a stable geologic formation, one that's deep below the earth's surface and isolated from any groundwater, in a place that's not prone to earthquakes or volcanoes. They want to dig the burial chamber out of rock that's not prone to fracturing under stress (such as salt or tuff) and/or that has the ability to bind chemically with and thus immobilize any radionuclides that somehow manage to escape from their packaging.

The place under Yucca Mountain where a deep burial chamber would go seems a likely site for several reasons. It's well above the current water table, it's in a bed of tuff (an appropriate sort of rock made from compacted volcanic ash), and it hasn't been violently shaken by earthquakes in at least 10,000 and possibly 100,000 years, according to a study financed by the Department of Energy.[21] Furthermore, Yucca Mountain is on the border of the Nevada Test Site, parts of which are heavily contaminated from years of nuclear weapons testing and must remain sealed off from public use.

Some geologists and many environmentalists have raised concerns about just how appropriate the site really is. Most of these concerns center on the difficulty of guessing what geologic changes might occur over the very long period—tens of thousands of years—that high-level wastes will remain dangerous. At the moment, the water table is low and rainfall is minimal at the site, but might this change? Is it really safe to rule out the likelihood of earthquakes or volcanoes? Furthermore, there may be very deep deposits of gas or oil beneath the site that could tempt future generations to drill or mine unknowingly into the waste burial site.

The testing and evaluation process at Yucca Mountain has been widely criticized. A 1993 General Accounting Office report found that only about 22 percent of what had thus far been spent on the project had gone for actual field studies; the rest of the money was eaten up by overhead and management costs.[22] The whole process has been astoundingly expensive. In 1992 the DOE estimated that it would end up costing about $6.5 billion just to evaluate the site.[23]

But the problem goes deeper than simple ineffi-
ciency and waste, critics say. Everyone involved in the
decision-making process has a strong incentive to put
the wastes at Yucca Mountain, strong enough to perhaps cloud the thinking about the site's suitability. The
government needs a waste repository and has no alternative to Yucca Mountain in sight. The contractors doing
the actual testing and evaluation will also be in the running to build and manage the facility.

If the DOE determines that Yucca Mountain is a
suitable site, it must then prepare a report on the project's environmental impact and send its recommenda-
tions to the president of the United States. If the president approves of the Yucca Mountain site, the proposal
will then go to Congress for approval. Nevada may veto
the site's selection, but Congress can override the state's
veto with a joint resolution. If the project gets Congress's approval, the DOE will then submit a design and
construction plan (one tailored to meet various Environmental Protection Agency requirements) to the Nuclear
Regulatory Commission. If it finds the plan satisfactory,
the NRC will issue a license to build the repository, and
construction will finally begin.

Once the repository is built, the tentative plan in
the mid-1990s was for the facility to accept wastes for
25 years, hold them so that they could be retrieved for
an additional 20 years, then decommission the facility,
decontaminate any areas that would remain accessible,
and permanently seal off the repository—which would
take five to twelve years more to complete.[24] Altogether,
the Yucca Mountain repository would hold up to
70,000 tons of high-level wastes, not only spent fuel

from commercial power plants but also high-level wastes from weapons production.[25]

As the planning and evaluation process has dragged on, the projected opening date for a repository at Yucca Mountain has receded farther and farther into the future. In March 1993 a scientific review board sponsored by Congress reported that no permanent underground facility could possibly be ready to accept high-level wastes by 2010 (at the time, that was the DOE's target date), and suggested that the whole program should be opened up for review.[26] By the end of 1993, DOE secretary Hazel O'Leary had said that 2013 was the earliest possible opening date.[27] The congressional General Accounting Office projected 2015 to 2023 instead.[28]

Since the DOE is obligated to start accepting spent fuel from civilian power reactors in 1998, clearly it will need to find a place to keep it until a permanent repository opens. The search is on for one or more temporary storage sites.

TEMPORARY MONITORED RETRIEVABLE STORAGE FACILITIES

The 1987 amendments to the Nuclear Waste Policy Act authorized the DOE to establish a temporary storage facility for spent fuel (a secure place in which to monitor the waste during the construction of its permanent burial ground) and offered money to any community that would accept such a facility. Although it is theoretically possible for the DOE to force such a facility on a community, the restrictions on doing so are so difficult that the DOE early on decided to rely on the voluntary process specified in the amendments, hoping that some community would find the money a strong enough incentive for hosting the storage site.

Beyond the obvious need for interim storage, there are several advantages to keeping high-level wastes in monitored, temporary storage for several decades. Much of the waste's heat and radioactivity would dissipate, making the waste much easier to handle when the time came to dispose of it permanently. Temporary storage would also buy time to research options for permanent disposal more thoroughly. There are disadvantages as well. Extra time would likely prolong the political wrangling over waste disposal. Further delays in making definitive plans for the waste would make accurate estimates of the ultimate cost of its disposal impossible to figure. Since disposal costs are part of the real cost of nuclear power, these costs would need to be known for any future consideration of whether to build more nuclear power plants. (For this reason, and because their waste problems are clearly finite, nations that have definitely decided to phase out nuclear power, such as Sweden, have found long-term temporary storage a more attractive option than the United States has.)

The most obvious sites for temporary storage are at the nuclear power plants. The spent fuel is already there, so there would be no need to transport it. Furthermore, even after the plants are decommissioned it may not be possible, or affordable, to decontaminate the plants completely. Since these radioactive places would have to remain under tight security for many years to come, why not secure the nuclear wastes there, as well?

Nuclear power plant operators and the communities around the plants are by and large uncomfortable with this line of reasoning. They fear that if spent fuel continues to pile up at the plants past the 1998 deadline, they may never be rid of it.

Similarly, with the future of Yucca Mountain still uncertain, few communities want to volunteer to host a temporary monitored retrievable storage (MRS) facility. Once wastes are gathered and secured at a "temporary" respository, the DOE might never develop a "permanent" alternative.

Nevertheless, a few communities have begun to investigate whether they might want to host an MRS site. Among them, ironically, is the displaced community of Bikini—the Pacific islanders evacuated in 1946 so that the United States could test nuclear bombs on their isolated cluster of islands. One of these islands, Nam, remains so badly contaminated by the 1954 Bravo hydrogen-bomb test that no cleanup has even been proposed. Bikinians have considered accepting an MRS facility there. MRS would bring in tens of millions of dollars each year—money the Bikinians could use in cleaning up and resettling themselves on their main island. However, few Bikinians are truly enthusiastic about this idea, and some are strongly opposed.[29] Furthermore, the practical problems of transporting high-level wastes so far would likely rule out the site, even if the islanders agreed to it.

Although the MRS siting process moved along faster than the Yucca Mountain project, it was clear by the early 1990s that no volunteer site would be ready in time to meet the 1998 deadline. By the end of 1992 the DOE was looking for temporary interim storage sites—

When this photo was taken at Bikini in 1949, researchers had been studying the effects of the atomic bomb tests of 1946 for three summers. The food supply was still contaminated, and researchers could not predict when the islanders could return.

places to hold the high-level wastes until an MRS facility is opened. The most likely candidates were existing federal facilities, especially weapons sites.

Two dozen or so local governments and Native American groups have considered hosting an MRS facility, including the Mescalero Apaches, whose home is in southern New Mexico, not far from the site of the 1945 Trinity bomb explosion.[30]

Why would anyone want to volunteer for MRS? Money. Congress recognized that it might take a great deal of money to buy a community's willingness to host such a concentration of radioactive wastes. Federal compensation to a host community could run as high as $50 million per year, in addition to whatever job opportunities and improved road and communication infrastructure the project might bring. According to Miller N. Hudson, the Mescalero Apaches' chief negotiator, "the federal government and the [nuclear] industry are ready to pour a huge bucket of money over any community that will take the monitored retrievable storage."[31]

Money notwithstanding, the tribe decided in early 1995 against an MRS facility. Their community had seemed the most likely candidate, and their decision makes it seem possible that an MRS facility will not be successfully sited anywhere in the United States.

MRS FOREVER?

Some scientists and others who have studied the issue believe that, instead of sealing off high-level wastes permanently, a better alternative would be to keep them accessible, where they could be monitored, perhaps at a *permanent* MRS facility at Yucca Mountain. Continuing to monitor the wastes at Yucca Mountain, and keeping them retrievable, would have several advantages. It would calm some of Nevada's opposition to the facility, it would allow for better environmental and defensive security, and it would allow more time to discover better disposal methods. If suitable technology develops, the wastes might someday be used for fuel or other purposes. [32]

Other people believe that it would be wrong to leave nuclear wastes for future generations to clean up and that we already have technology and an understanding of the problem that are adequate to handle permanent disposal safely. Furthermore, some geologic evidence suggests that permanent deep burial, in the right location, *can* work. Some 2 billion years ago in West Africa, near what is now the village of Oklo, in Gabon, a very rich uranium deposit spontaneously underwent nuclear fission reactions. Since then, most of the fission products and nearly all of the long-lived transuranic elements have remained in place, moving no more than 6 feet (1.8 meters) from where they were formed so many years ago. [33]

The problem, as one scientist has put it, "is not of digging a hole in the ground; it's of forecasting the future." [34] We've set 10,000 years as the amount of time a "permanent" waste facility would need to be secure (although some radioisotopes in high-level waste will remain dangerous for hundreds of thousands of years), and that is a very long time. How confident can we be not only that we've correctly predicted the geologic future, but also that current packaging and sealing technology will withstand the test of this stretch of time?

Not just geology and technology must be considered, but human nature as well. Kai Erikson, a social scientist, makes an eloquent case that even if we could vouch for Yucca Mountain's geologic security for the next 10,000 years, the notion that we could predict what humans might do that would affect the site is absurd. "It is difficult to predict what human beings will do a year hence," Erikson has written, "hard even to guess what they will do a decade hence, but preposterous to think that one can even begin to know what they will do a century or a millennium hence."[35] Consider that 10,000 ago our ancestors' technology was that of the Stone Age.

Erikson believes that it's likely that the cultural and technological gap between us and our descendants will be even greater than the gap between us and our stone-wielding ancestors, because the pace of technological change so far has accelerated fairly steadily. How can we guess what our descendants might wish to excavate at Yucca Mountain, or what tools they might use for the digging? "What are the odds," Erikson wonders, "that a mineral for which no one can imagine any use will come to be seen as valuable enough to be worth the risking of lives? Uranium had no known uses as recently as one hundred years ago."

How are we to warn our descendants 10,000 years into the future? Erikson suggests that it might be best to devise some way for the message to be revised with every generation, to reflect changes in language and in mind-set. The true challenge, he says, is to make sure not only that the message isn't forgotten but also that it doesn't become dangerously distorted:

> The danger is not so much that the warning system will fail to alert a future civilization but that it will do so all too well. Some people may come to believe that a powerful weapon lies buried out there in the middle of enemy territory, waiting only to be activated. Some may come to believe that the remains of an ancient culture lie buried out there in the middle of a new one, set in the deepest tombs the age could dig and protected by a mysterious curse. What curiosity might that excite? Some may come to believe that a thing of supernatural force and energy lies buried out there in the middle of the desert, crowned by monuments so large and exuberant that they cry out for attention. What religious awe might that inspire?

CHAPTER FOUR
NUCLEAR WEAPONS
PRODUCTION

It takes a very strong
head to keep secrets for years,
and not go slightly mad.

C. P. SNOW [1]

From the beginning, the extreme secrecy surrounding the U.S. nuclear weapons program hid carelessness in the handling of wastes. For example, during the early days of the Manhattan Project, untreated liquid radioactive wastes were simply dumped into the canyons around the bomb assembly complex at Los Alamos. [2]

After World War II, as the Cold War arms buildup got under way, a disturbing pattern developed. The government would set production goals for nuclear weapons, often very high ones, and leave it up to defense contractors to figure out how to meet them. Contractors were rewarded with bonuses and more contracts if they met their goals, and the government usually took the contractors' word that work was being done safely. (Actually, the government never had enough inspectors to check up on the contractors' operations.) This system encouraged contractors to cut corners, since no money was to be made (and money possibly could be lost) from adhering to strict health, safety, and environmental standards. In the push to meet production goals, nuclear wastes were often handled haphazardly, and workers' health and safety were endangered.

Reports of accidents sometimes seeped into the press. These reports, in the context of the general information blackout surrounding weapons facilities, led more and more Americans to suspect that their government was hiding the hazards of nuclear weaponry behind a curtain of national security. The suspicion that the public wasn't being told the whole story contributed to a widespread mistrust that continues even today of government proposals concerning nuclear technology, including ones that deal with nuclear wastes.

In a perfect world, all of the radioactive materials that pass through or are created within a nuclear facility would ultimately end up as a useful product or as a minimal amount of waste carefully isolated and packaged for safe disposal. In the real world, however, some radioactivity escapes and contaminates the environment outside as well as inside every nuclear facility. Health, safety, and environmental regulations are supposed to minimize this contamination and clean it up when it occurs. Years of lax standards at U.S. weapons facilities have allowed a great deal of contamination to endanger workers and the public, and have created expensive cleanup problems and an unnecessarily large amount of hard-to-handle radioactive waste. Two facilities with especially nasty records of contamination are the bomb-making plant at Rocky Flats, Colorado, and the Hanford, Washington, plutonium works.

ROCKY FLATS

The weapons facility at Rocky Flats made plutonium triggers for nuclear warheads and thus handled large quantities of plutonium. In addition to its radioactive properties, plutonium has the unusual chemical property of being prone to burst spontaneously into flame. Over the years many small fires at Rocky Flats released plutonium into the atmosphere. A catastrophic fire occurred in 1969. Fortunately for the residents of nearby Denver, the building's roof remained intact. Cleanup costs ran to tens of millions of dollars.

In 1974 the U.S. Environmental Protection Agency (EPA) documented that cattle in a pasture east of Rocky Flats were more contaminated with plutonium than cattle set out to graze on the government's Nevada nuclear weapons test site. Since then, the federal government has bought up thousands of acres of contaminated land around Rocky Flats to prevent its use by the public. But the wind has continued to blow dust from that land onto inhabited areas around Denver. In 1981 a doctor's study associated higher than expected cancer rates with the areas around Rocky Flats most contaminated with plutonium. By the late 1980s, radioactive

No longer in operation, the Rocky Flats nuclear weapons plant had been plagued with problems, including contamination in the area around the plant and safety deficiencies inside the plant. A grand jury trial ended in a plea bargain in 1992 by Rockwell International, the corporation contracted to run the plant.

[67]

and other toxic wastes from Rocky Flats that had leached into groundwater were threatening Denver's water supply.[3]

Inside the plant, conditions were even worse. In 1988 a government inspector found workers at Rocky Flats handling radioactive materials without adequate protective clothing and then—without being checked for contamination—going directly to the lunchroom, where they ate lunch with dozens of their coworkers. Procedures for the disposing of contaminated rags and other waste were equally lax. The Department of Energy (DOE) ordered that key operations at the plant be shut down due to safety deficiencies.[4]

Problems at the plant continued. By 1989 the *Washington Post* reported that 62 pounds (approximately 28 kilograms) of plutonium had gotten past air filters and accumulated in the plant's air ducts, prompting concern that enough might have clumped together somewhere in the ductwork to "go critical"—release an intense burst of radioactivity in a nuclear chain reaction. That fall, the DOE shut down the whole plant "temporarily," for safety improvements. At the end of that year, the DOE canceled Rockwell International's contract to run the plant.[5]

Meanwhile, in June 1989, Federal Bureau of Investigation and EPA agents raided Rocky Flats, looking for evidence of environmental crimes. This investigation extended for years and ended in 1992 with a plea bargain. Rockwell admitted to five felonies and five misdemeanors, and agreed to pay an $18.5 million fine.[6]

The grand jurors who had spent two and a half years hearing the evidence in this investigation cried foul. They publicly charged that the U.S. Justice Department, whose prosecutors had negotiated the plea bargain with Rockwell, had prevented the grand jury from pressing the case to a just conclusion. They wanted the government not only to indict specific individuals at Rockwell (only the corporation itself, not individuals, had admitted to wrongdoing in the plea bargain) but also to consider indictments against the DOE. The grand jury report on the investigation asserted:

> The DOE explicitly discouraged Rockwell from complying with environmental laws by omitting environmental compliance for [sic] the list of criteria according to which large performance bonus fees were paid to Rockwell during the period from 1985 through 1989. Significantly, these large financial incentives (which were in the millions of dollars) could be earned most easily if Rockwell ignored environmental compliance in striving to meet weapons-production goals.[7]

Rebellious grand jurors notwithstanding, the plea bargain held.

Today, the Rocky Flats plant no longer operates. The nuclear waste and contamination it generated, however, will remain for years to come.

HANFORD

The Hanford Reservation, located along the Columbia River in the state of Washington, began producing plutonium for nuclear weapons during World War II. From the beginning, waste disposal was haphazard at Hanford. Pressed for time during the war, Hanford's engineers decided simply to dump low-level wastes on the reservation and into the Columbia River, expecting the environment to dilute them. High-level wastes were stored "temporarily"; the engineers expected they'd figure out what to do with them after the war. (They didn't. As of 1995, high-level wastes remained in tanks on the reservation.) As early as 1948, the Atomic Energy Commission's (AEC) Committee on Nuclear Safety recommended that Hanford change its disposal methods, which included pits designed to permit low-level wastes to seep into the ground and corrosion-prone single-wall tanks for high-level wastes. The AEC didn't implement the recommended changes, partly, it said, because it didn't have enough money to do so.[8]

During Hanford's peak years, nine nuclear reactors operated at the reservation. Waste disposal and storage continued to be haphazard. In 1965 gas pressure in one of the high-level waste tanks shot a radioactive geyser 50 feet (15 meters) into the air.[9] Safety procedures were often haphazard, and sometimes workers got hurt. The best-known case of worker injury was that of Harold McCluskey, the "Atomic Man." A 1976 explosion shot hundreds of contaminated glass shards into the 64-year-old worker. Miraculously, he survived. Years after the accident, McCluskey could still set off a Geiger counter set 50 feet away. (He died, apparently of natural causes, at age 75.)[10]

The 1986 disaster at the Soviet nuclear weapons facility at Chernobyl sent shock waves through the American nuclear weapons production establishment.

Radiation monitoring at the Chernobyl nuclear power plant after its notorious accident in 1986.

This is one of the first pictures taken inside the Chernobyl complex, five years after the meltdown. Researchers are measuring the level of radioactivity at the crater's edge where the reactor was located.

Chernobyl also spurred increased demands from antinuclear activists, and from the press, for more information about how the U.S. nuclear facilities were being operated. Suddenly, plant safety seemed more important. "Chernobyl broke the log jam," DOE secretary John Harrington later recalled. "Everything we had started to do in terms of safety and the environment was speeded up."[11]

Environmental and safety audits at plants all over the United States revealed major problems, and the DOE closed or suspended operations at plant after plant in 1986, 1987, and 1988. Hanford's last remaining active reactor, the N Reactor, shut down after Chernobyl. In 1988 the DOE made that shutdown permanent after concluding that it could get all the plutonium it needed, and get it more cheaply, from its Savannah River, Georgia, plant.

The chief controversy concerning Hanford during that time was not fear that a Chernobyl-style catastrophe might happen. Instead, concern was focused on a catastrophe that already *had* occurred: the release of radiation into the environment around Hanford during the many years of its operation.

In 1986 and 1987, Hanford officials released tens of thousands of pages of documents concerning Hanford's operations over the years. The biggest bombshell in these documents was information about the Green Run—an experimental nuclear reactor run that in 1949 had released 11,000 curies of radioactivity into the air at Hanford. (By contrast, the accident at Three Mile Island released only 15 curies.)[12] Most of Hanford's radioactive emissions, from the Green Run and from more normal operations, were iodine 131, which causes thyroid problems.

[73]

In 1987 the U.S. Centers for Disease Control reported that people who had lived downwind from Hanford were quite possibly the most irradiated citizens in the United States, and that they were much more likely to experience certain radiation-related diseases. Those who as children had drunk contaminated milk were especially at risk; many developed thyroid tumors and other disorders. (In 1990 a preliminary report from the DOE's Dose Reconstruction Project demonstrated that some of the children around Hanford had been dosed with more radiation than children caught in Chernobyl's cloud.) By 1993, thousands of Hanford *"downwinders"* with radiation-related illnesses had signed onto a lawsuit against the companies that, as the government's chief contractors, had been responsible for running Hanford.[13]

CHANGING THE RULES

In 1989 the DOE began to make comprehensive plans for consolidating its operations and closing some weapons facilities. It also started on an ambitious 30-year program to clean up the wastes and health and environmental hazards that had accumulated over decades of nuclear weapons production. In 1992, President George Bush canceled the only remaining nuclear warheads still in production. The nuclear arms race was over, but the cleanup had just begun.

The cleanup will be governed by much stricter standards than in the early years of the arms race. The 1954 Atomic Energy Act not only shrouded nuclear

Two children being treated for radiation-related illnesses in 1991 in Minsk — the accident at Chernobyl had leaked radiation into Belorussia where they were living.

weapons production in secrecy but also explicitly exempted it from most environmental, health, and labor regulations. Well into the 1980s the DOE continued to claim that national security concerns made the weapons program exempt from the flurry of environmental legislation passed in the 1970s.

That changed in 1984, when a lawsuit against the DOE brought by the Natural Resources Defense Council and the Legal Environmental Assistance Foundation (*LEAF* v. *Hodel*) compelled the DOE to acknowledge that federal environmental laws (and some state and local regulations as well) govern its weapons production activities. Important federal laws that now govern the weapons facilities include:

• *The 1969 National Environmental Policy Act (NEPA)*, which requires environmental impact statements for all DOE activities.

• *The federal Clean Air and Clean Water Acts*, which direct the EPA to set standards for radioactive emissions for both DOE facilities and commercial nuclear power plants.

• *The 1976 Resource Conservation and Recovery Act (RCRA)*, which governs hazardous and other solid wastes, though not specifically radioactive wastes. Weapons plants generate a lot of mixed wastes (radioactive materials mixed with other hazardous wastes) that are subject to RCRA's requirements to reduce the volume of such wastes and to handle them in ways that meet EPA approval.

• *Superfund (the 1980 Comprehensive Environmental Response, Compensation, and Liability Act)*, which requires government or civilian polluters (including the DOE) to clean up hazardous or radioactive contamination that threatens the public or the environment. Several weapons facilities are on Superfund's National Priorities List.

• *The* 1992 *Federal Facilities Compliance Act* (FFCA), which makes federal facilities, including the DOE's, subject to the same punishment as private industry if they violate environmental laws. Although FFCA is potentially a very powerful tool for environmental lawsuits, its ultimate impact is not yet clear.

A NEW DOE?

In the past the DOE often has been very slow to comply with health, safety, and environmental standards. The department, which is contractually obligated to pay the legal fees of its nuclear weapons contractors, has been more inclined to fight than to settle lawsuits brought by workers and civilians claiming to have been harmed by exposure to radiation from DOE sites. Between 1991 and 1993, the DOE spent $50 million on lawyers' fees in eight such cases. (The most expensive case, at $20.2 million in fees during those years, involves the residents, business owners, and veterans who have filed suit against contractors at Hanford.)[14]

In 1993, however, the DOE's new secretary, Hazel O'Leary, began to open up the DOE to public scrutiny and to act on a new commitment to give safety, health, and environmental concerns top priority during the cleanup of weapons sites. To ensure worker safety during the cleanup, the DOE voluntarily put its operations under federal Occupational Safety and Health Administration (OSHA) regulations and supervision.[15] And to ensure greater public access to information about DOE operations, Secretary O'Leary renamed and gave a new mission to the department's Office of Classification, which had been responsible for labeling department documents "classified" (secret for security reasons). Brian Siebert, director of the new Office of Declassification, explained its agenda: "What is going on here is more than just changing the labels on documents. It is lifting the veil of secrecy that has hung over us since the Cold War."[16]

CHAPTER FIVE
CLEANING UP AFTER
THE ARMS RACE

Weeks *after* George Bush was elected president, in 1988, his designated budget director, Richard Darman, visited outgoing energy secretary John S. Herrington to talk about environmental cleanup at the Department of Energy's (DOE) weapons facilities.

"Well, just how bad is this thing?" Darman asked. "How much is it going to cost?"

"Dick," the secretary answered, "it's going to take everything you've got."[1]

Secretary Herrington was not exaggerating. A 1991 report by Congress's Office of Technology Assessment found evidence that "air, groundwater, surface water, sediments, and soil, as well as vegetation and wildlife, have been contaminated at most, if not all, of the Department of Energy nuclear weapons sites."[2]

In the earliest days of the Nuclear Age, sites no longer needed for bomb development were decommissioned and released for other uses. Cleanup at these sites wasn't always up to modern standards. Later, in the 1970s, the federal government slated 33 of these sites in 13 states for further cleanup. (By the end of 1992, cleanup had been completed at only 11 locations.)[3] In 1989 the DOE set the far from realistic goal (affirmed by Congress in 1991) of completing environmental cleanup at all of its nuclear sites within thirty years.

The United States has produced no new nuclear weapons since 1992 and is committed to sharply reducing its nuclear arsenal in the years ahead. The DOE's mission has shifted from creating weapons-grade uranium and plutonium and building weapons to dismantling weapons and cleaning up the bomb factories. Taking stock of the problem in 1992, the DOE determined that nuclear waste and nuclear contamination had accumulated at more than 100 sites in 36 states and U.S. territories. In the summer of 1993, the DOE assistant secretary in charge of the cleanup estimated that cleanup costs could reach as high as $1 trillion.[4] No matter how much money is spent, it's likely that many sites will never be sufficiently decontaminated for unrestricted use.

LOW-LEVEL WASTES

Several sorts of low-level wastes have been generated by the nuclear weapons program:

• Soil and other materials contaminated by weapons testing, especially at the Nevada test site. Since most tests were conducted underground, most of this waste is buried and not retrievable. It is, however, necessary to continue to monitor these wastes to make sure that they remain sealed off from the public and don't contaminate groundwater.

• Low-level wastes from running nuclear reactors to produce plutonium and from other weapons plants activities. Since new plutonium for bombs is not being produced, this stream of waste has dwindled. In the past, such wastes were shipped to government-owned dumps (some of which now require cleanup) or kept at the weapons facilities where they were produced.

• Low-level wastes from decommissioning and decontaminating weapons facilities. In the years ahead, this cleanup will generate a huge volume of low-level waste, ranging from the contents of old dumps that must be moved to contaminated rubble from dismantled buildings.

Low-level wastes from the weapons program are scattered all over the United States. The question of what to do with all this material—stabilize it and seal it off, or cart it away to someplace else—has generated much controversy in the communities around some of these sites. As the DOE's cleanup progresses, wastes will be consolidated at fewer sites, most likely at larger facilities that are already badly contaminated, such as the Hanford complex, New Mexico's Los Alamos National Laboratory, the Idaho National Engineering Lab (INEL), and the Oak Ridge and Savannah River facilities in the Southeast. Due to the sloppy handling over many years of wastes at weapons facilities, cleaning up the mess will in many cases be difficult and expensive.

TRANSURANIC AND
MIXED WASTES

To make nuclear weapons, technicians at various weapons facilities took spent fuel from nuclear reactors, combined it with chemicals to separate out certain elements, then extracted the desirable plutonium and uranium. Deriving weapons-grade plutonium and uranium from spent fuel is messy and hazardous, and it generates several problematic categories of waste: transuranic waste and mixed waste. Transuranic waste is a catchall category similar to low-level waste except that it is contaminated with the heavier-than-uranium elements that are created inside a working nuclear reactor; many of these elements are, like plutonium, very long-lived and very toxic. Mixed waste is similar waste that includes hazardous chemicals. Scientists don't completely understand just how the radioactive elements in mixed waste interact with these chemicals, and how the results of these interactions make the waste more hazardous.

Before 1970, transuranic and mixed wastes from the weapons programs were not separated from low-level nuclear wastes and were buried along with them at half a dozen federal sites. Since 1970, weapons facilities have been required to separate transuranic and mixed wastes from low-level wastes and to take steps to reduce their volume.

To deal with mixed wastes that are not contaminated with transuranic elements, the DOE has pursued a controversial policy of incinerating these wastes—burning off the hazardous chemicals—then disposing of the ash as low-level waste. Environmentalists and community activists worry about the hazardous substances that might be emitted from such an incinerator's smoke-stack. Incinerators have been put into operation or planned at the DOE's Oak Ridge, Savannah River, INEL, and Los Alamos facilities.[5]

As for transuranic wastes, most of the volume and nearly all of the radioactivity of these wastes are stored at just a few weapons facilities. (Not included in this tally are the transuranic wastes buried at the low-level waste dumps before 1970; it's not yet clear how much of that waste will stay where it is and how much will be dug up and relocated.) As of 1993, INEL held 60 percent of the volume of these stored wastes but only about 20 percent of their radioactivity. Transuranic wastes at Savannah River and Oak Ridge accounted for only about 10 percent of the stored wastes' total volume but were much more intensely radioactive, accounting for 70 percent of the total radioactivity.[6] Although most transuranic wastes have little penetrating radiation and are thus easy to handle, they include radioisotopes that will remain extremely dangerous for anyone to ingest during the next 10,000 or even 100,000 years or more—essentially forever. The DOE intends to bury its transuranic wastes permanently at the Waste Isolation Pilot Project.

WASTE ISOLATION PILOT PROJECT

The Waste Isolation Pilot Project (WIPP) is a cavernous burial site dug out of salt deposits 2,150 feet (655 meters) below the ground near Carlsbad, New Mexico. Since 1975, when it was first decided to locate WIPP at this site, WIPP has been the subject of much political

A test shaft at the Waste Isolation Pilot Project (WIPP) in which a continuous mining machine mines salt at the rate of 300 tons per hour.

wrangling, and its mission has been altered several times. It has returned to its original purpose as a permanent burial ground for the weapons program's transuranic wastes. Since WIPP can hold as much as 220 million cubic feet (6.25 million cubic meters), however— far more than the volume of transuranic wastes now in storage—the temptation to bury additional sorts of waste at WIPP may be difficult to resist.

Although WIPP's construction is fairly well completed, evaluation, testing, and planning for the project continue. A final decision about moving all the stored transuranic wastes to WIPP will probably not be made until after the turn of the century. The project is well behind schedule and much more expensive than originally budgeted. By 1993, $1.5 billion had been spent on WIPP; it's likely that an additional $1.5 billion will be spent by the year 2000.[7]

Many environmentalists believe that WIPP is fatally flawed. Its burial chambers are dug out of a salt deposit that is sandwiched between a pressurized brine reservoir below and a freshwater aquifer that feeds the Pecos River above. Water seeps through the salt walls of the burial chambers, and this briny liquid could corrode the steel drums in which transuranic wastes are stored. Worse still, the wastes give off gases that could build up pressure after the site is sealed, open up cracks in the salt deposits, and force contaminated material up into the aquifer above. "We believe that a truly comprehensive review [of WIPP] would yield a termination as opposed to going forward," says Scott Denman, executive director of Safe Energy Communication Council, a coalition of environmental organizations that opposes the project.[8] But with so much money already spent on WIPP, and no place else to put the wastes, the DOE is very strongly motivated to go forward.

HIGH-LEVEL WASTES

Just as spent fuel has been piling up with no place to go at civilian nuclear power reactors, so has it been piling up at weapons facilities. Both civilian and military spent fuel are ultimately to be sent to the same permanent disposal facility—Yucca Mountain, if the site is approved.

Some of this high-level waste is very much like civilian spent fuel. For example, spent fuel from the Navy's nuclear submarines used to be reprocessed at INEL to get uranium and plutonium; now, with uranium cheap and plentiful and plutonium no longer needed, the spent fuel is stored there as high-level waste. (Idaho has been wary of this practice, both because INEL's environmental record has been dismal and because, with no alternatives in sight, Idaho has feared that the site may become a de facto long-term high-level waste repository. As of 1994, however, shipments of the Navy's spent fuel to INEL continued.)[9]

Some spent fuel was also left in limbo as reactors at Hanford, Savannah River, and INEL were shut down for safety reasons in the 1980s. Spent fuel from reactors at these facilities used to be left to cool in pools of water (so-called "swimming pools") for a year or so before being reprocessed to separate out plutonium and uranium for weapons. When the facilities were shut down, spent fuel remained in the pools, even though the pools were not designed for long-term storage. By the end of 1993, some containers of spent fuel had rusted through, contaminating the surrounding water with radioactivity. Some of the pools themselves appeared to be leaking.[10]

But gruesome as these swimming pools sound, they are a relatively simple problem compared with the DOE's most troublesome high-level wastes: those left from reprocessing spent fuel to remove weapons-grade isotopes. During reprocessing, the highly radioactive

[86]

spent fuel was dissolved in corrosive chemicals. After the desired plutonium and uranium were removed, a nasty, extremely dangerous stew of various radioactive isotopes and toxic chemicals remained.

These high-level wastes have been treated differently at different DOE facilities. At INEL, the highly acidic wastes were first poured into stainless steel vats. Beginning in the 1960s this waste was evaporated and converted into dry granules that are now stored in underground concrete bins. Because it is dry and relatively stable, this INEL waste is the least of the DOE's high-level waste problems.

At Hanford and Savannah River, sodium hydroxide was poured into the raw, acidic wastes to neutralize them before they were pumped into huge steel tanks. This not only increased the volume of the wastes but also precipitated a sludge of unknown chemical composition out of the liquid wastes. This sludge has gummed up the interior of the tanks. Over the years, the tanks have corroded, and thousands of gallons of radioactive liquid have leaked from them, seeping into the ground at Hanford and Savannah River. Furthermore, chemical reactions have created flammable gases in many of the tanks. From time to time tanks "belch," releasing large flammable puffs of accumulated gas that have the potential to cause a catastrophic explosion.

The DOE has decided that the best way to dispose of high-level wastes left over from reprocessing will be to "vitrify" it (embed it in glass) and then entomb it, most likely at Yucca Mountain. *Vitrification* not only casts the waste into a solid form that's easier to handle and safer to transport but also immobilizes the radioactivity. Embedded in glass, the radioactive wastes won't

DEFENSE WASTE PROCESSING FACILITY MELTER AND TURNTABLE

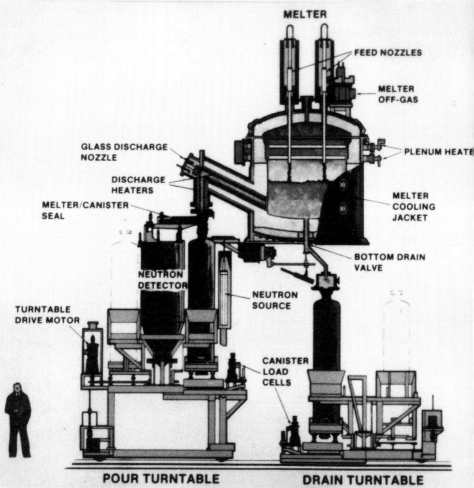

This chart from the Department of Energy demonstrates the vitrification process for high-level waste.

leach out even if water washes through their burial site in the distant future.

There are two problems with vitrification, however. One is that the process is very expensive. (That's why high-level wastes from America's nuclear power plants aren't slated for vitrification.) The other problem is that the liquid wastes at Hanford and Savannah River present a host of technical difficulties. Some of the problems are mechanical—how to pump the dangerous and lumpy stew safely out of the tanks. Other problems are chemical—nobody knows the exact composition of what's in all those tanks and no one can predict how their contents will behave during vitrification. For example, in 1993 the vitrification project at Savannah River, then running five years late and $1 billion over budget, was at a standstill while scientists worked to solve the latest technical hitch. Wastes that were sent to a chemical processing plant to be prepared for vitrification were unexpectedly giving off a dangerous chemical.[11]

HANFORD—A SLEW OF PROBLEMS

Easily the worst of the DOE's problems with nuclear wastes of all kinds are at Hanford. The Hanford Reservation is one of the oldest and largest of the nation's nuclear weapons facilities. At 560 square miles (approximately 1,450 square kilometers), Hanford is half the size of the state of Rhode Island. Hanford produced plutonium for nuclear weapons from 1943 until 1988, and it is home to nearly two thirds of the weapons program's total volume of solid and liquid hazardous and radioactive wastes, including 65 million gallons (more than 245 million liters) of high-level reprocessing wastes stored in 177 underground tanks. In addition, about 440 *billion* gallons (approximately 1.7 trillion liters) of other wastes have been leached into the ground at Hanford over the years. At least 100 square miles (260 square kilometers), possibly much more, of groundwater have been contaminated with *radionuclides* and hazardous chemicals; radionuclides from Hanford have been detected 200 miles (322 kilometers) downstream in the Columbia River, which runs by Hanford and is fed by groundwater beneath the reservation. Cleaning up Hanford is expected to cost more than $57 billion and to take longer than thirty years.[12]

Nuclear wastes have been dumped at more than 1,400 locations on the Hanford Reservation. Although the wastes include enough plutonium to build perhaps two dozen nuclear weapons, most of the volume of what has been dumped consists of low-level wastes ranging from workers' contaminated clothing to contaminated heavy equipment, such as bulldozers. It is even rumored that workers on the reservation once laid track into a pit into which an irradiated locomotive was driven and buried.[13] The waste records at Hanford are haphazard, especially for the early years, so nobody knows exactly what's there, or even all the places where waste has been buried.

In May 1993, after years of argument, government officials, environmentalists, scientific experts, and representatives of Native American tribes and other local interests agreed on an overall cleanup strategy for Hanford. DOE contractors were to move hazardous materials from all over the reservation into a smaller zone, the "200 Area," where the tanks of high-level wastes are buried. This section is so badly contaminated that it may never be completely cleaned up. The 200 Area is to be a *temporary* storage site for the transported hazardous wastes; a permanent solution has not yet been determined. Concentrating wastes in the 200 Area will allow cleanup to proceed more quickly, it is hoped, on the rest of the reservation.[14]

The thorniest problem in the 200 Area is the leakage in the underground tanks. Every year another two or three of the huge steel tanks, which weren't designed for long-term use, begin to leak into the surrounding soil. By mid-1993, 68 of the 177 tanks were on the DOE's list of "assumed leakers."[15] This leakage has amounted to more than 1 million gallons (3.8 million liters), in addition to the unknown quantity of liquid that in years past was routinely siphoned off from the tanks and dumped on the ground.[16]

The scariest aspect of the tanks isn't leakage; it's the threat that gases bubbling up in the tanks might ignite. An explosion of similar waste tanks in the Soviet Union in the 1950s spewed radioactive contamination over thousands of square miles in the southern Ural Mountains. More recently, in April 1993, a waste tank holding a brew similar to what's kept at Hanford exploded at the Russian reprocessing plant at Tomsk-7.

Efforts to forestall such a disaster at Hanford have been mixed. On the one hand, in July 1993 an elaborate $30 million mixing pump was installed in the tank considered the most dangerous. The theory behind the mixer was to bleed the tank's gases off steadily, rather than letting large bubbles build up to be emitted in dangerous "burps." (Technicians timed the installation for shortly after the tank had burped thousands of cubic feet of hydrogen.)[17] Other efforts to cope with the tanks have been slipshod. For example, just a few weeks after the high-tech mixing pump was installed, a Hanford worker was contaminated with radioactive wastes after lowering a rock on a rope into one of the tanks, to check if one of the tank's pipes was blocked.[18]

Concerned about the Tomsk-7 explosion, the U.S. Senate's Governmental Affairs Committee looked into the matter and reported that such a disaster might indeed be possible at Hanford. "The potential risk here in the United States is real and widespread," according to the committee's chairman, Senator John Glenn.[19]

Assuming that Hanford continues to avoid such a catastrophe, the problem of disposing the waste in the tanks remains. Construction of the vitrification plant at Hanford was suspended in April 1993; the state of Washington, the DOE, and the Environmental Protection Agency cited technical problems.[20] There have been political problems as well. Early plans called for the wastes in the tanks to be separated. The most hazardous part of the wastes was to be vitrified then shipped to the permanent high-level waste burial facility tentatively sited at Yucca Mountain. The remainder was to be mixed into concrete, then poured into giant vaults and left at Hanford. The public, however, rebelled at the idea of the concrete vaults. Eventually, it was decided to vitrify *all* of the wastes in the tanks, even though this would create about 38,000 glass logs, 10 feet long by 2 feet wide (approximately 300 by 60 centimeters). This is more than there'll be room for at Yucca Mountain. At the end of 1993, plans were drawn up calling for building and operating a larger-capacity vitrification plant, then sending only the vitrified highly radioactive sludge to Yucca Mountain and keeping the vitrified remnant at Hanford. The whole process is to be completed by 2028—assuming that all of the project's technical hurdles are overcome and that Yucca Mountain is selected and readied by then.[21]

CLEANUP OR BOONDOGGLE?

By the early 1990s the DOE was spending more than $1 billion each year at Hanford. That is more money than was spent when the plant was actually making weapons. Nearly all of this money was being spent on planning rather than on actual cleanup operations.[22] Meanwhile, conditions at Hanford were becoming more, not less, hazardous. An internal DOE report dated July 1992 stated that the Hanford cleanup was failing; in particular, it said, efforts to stabilize the tanks weren't keeping up with their deterioration.[23]

Safety problems aren't unique to Hanford. A 1992 surprise inspection at the DOE's Portsmouth Gaseous Diffusion Plant in Ohio, for example, turned up 578 health and safety violations, according to an aide to Senator Glenn.[24]

Persistent safety problems raise the question of whether money for the weapons cleanup is being wisely spent. It certainly has been lavishly spent. A 1993 DOE study showed that the department was paying its contractors one third more to clean up nuclear sites than private industry pays for similar projects. What is worse is that this expensive work was usually completed late, and that more than half of the contracts studied generated cost overruns.[25]

[93]

CHAPTER SIX
THE PROBLEM
OF PLUTONIUM

The end of the Cold War arms race created a whole new category of nuclear waste: decommissioned nuclear weapons. It's relatively easy to take highly enriched uranium (HEU, 90 to 95 percent pure) from these weapons and dilute it to make fuel for civilian nuclear power plants. Once diluted, to a concentration of less than 5 percent, the uranium can't be used for weapons without once again going through elaborate and expensive enrichment processing. In 1993, Princeton University's Center for Energy and Environmental Studies estimated that enough HEU existed, around the world, to fuel all of the world's nuclear power reactors for two years.[1] At that time, however, the United States was still stockpiling HEU from dismantled weapons rather than blending it down. Russia, however, had begun to turn some of its HEU into nuclear fuel, some of which was sold to U.S. power plants.

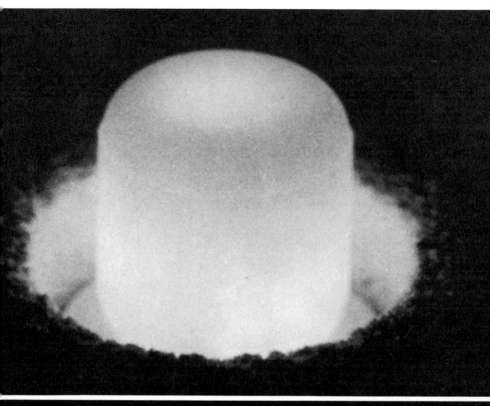

A glowing plutonium-238 sphere.

Plutonium from the weapons program is a knottier problem. It is an exceedingly potent explosive. Just a few pounds of plutonium, a piece about the size of a large grapefruit, can easily be fashioned into a crude nuclear weapon. Furthermore, although plutonium is highly toxic and will remain so for thousands of years, its radiation isn't very intense, so it can be safely handled and easily smuggled without elaborate shielding. Plutonium is a would-be nuclear terrorist's dream weapon, and an unshakable military security nightmare. No nation that possesses plutonium can afford to lose track of even a tiny amount.

The United States has accumulated at least 33.5 tons of plutonium at seven weapons facilities, mostly in the western part of the country. An additional 55.5 tons are, or were, contained in America's nuclear weapons.[2] Dismantling most of these weapons is a huge project that ultimately will cost somewhere between $500 million and $1 billion.[3] This process is already under way at the Department of Energy's Pantex facility.

PANTEX

Built during World War II, Pantex covers 16,000 acres (6,500 hectares) in the Texas Panhandle. Pantex began to produce nuclear weapons in 1951; by 1994, workers at the facility were dismantling them at the rate of 1,400 to 2,000 per year.

The great danger in disassembling a nuclear weapon isn't a nuclear explosion. Scientists say an explosion can't happen accidentally because of the way bombs are constructed. Instead, what is feared is that the conventional chemical explosives that surround the fissionable elements in a nuclear device could ignite and disperse the bomb's radioactive materials. Disassembly crews work in fortified underground rooms called "gravel gerties." The rooms are round, according to a reporter who toured the facility, so that if there is a nonnuclear explosion, the blast would be directed upward, where it would raise the roof, which is covered to a depth of 15.5 feet [4.73 meters] with sand and gravel. Then the gravel would come back down and crash through the roof, snuffing out the explosion, and incidentally the eight or ten technicians in the room. "It wouldn't matter to them," a plant official [explained]. . . . "They wouldn't be alive to notice."[4]

Disassembly technicians are very, very careful workers. Many have said that they are also very pleased to be taking bombs apart rather than putting them together, as was done at Pantex for so many years.

Some residents of the area are more wary about the project. Pantex's environmental record is less than pristine. In 1994 the complex was placed on the federal Superfund's list of sites urgently needing cleanup.[5] People near Pantex worry that as more plutonium accumulates there "temporarily," the government may decide that it's too risky to move it elsewhere. Thousands of bombs have been dismantled at Pantex, and the bowling-ball-size plutonium "pit" from each weapon has remained on-site, since the DOE has no place else to put it. By 1993 it was obvious that Pantex would run out of storage space for the plutonium pits well before work would be completed on the 15,000 or so weapons slated for dismantling. The DOE has promised to complete a detailed study of the environmental implications of continuing to store plutonium pits at Pantex; no more than 12,000 pits are to accumulate there until the study is done.[6]

[97]

PLUTONIUM OPTIONS

What *can* be done with all this plutonium? Pits can be shaped into metal ingots or otherwise altered to make them useless as weapons without expensive refabrication. Storing plutonium in this form is the simplest way to meet our commitment to decommission nuclear weapons. Metal plutonium, however, is flammable and thus risky to store even if it is treated to minimize the danger of fire. Alternatively, the plutonium pits can be chemically changed into an oxide powder before storage. This is a messy process, but the powder is safer and easier to handle. Moreover, it can't be used for weapons without a costly and difficult chemical reconversion.

To answer the security concerns raised by plutonium, some observers have suggested burying it in holes several *miles* deep, deep enough to be both unretrievable and isolated from the biosphere. Others suggest storing it with very hot spent reactor fuel, so that anyone attempting to steal the plutonium would be fatally burned. The same principle could be applied to *permanent* disposal: Mix the plutonium with spent fuel, vitrify it, and bury it.

Another option is to use plutonium as fuel for civilian power reactors. This would have the advantage of actually destroying the plutonium, but also the disadvantage of creating a new stream of high-level wastes. (Spent fuel, although it doesn't present plutonium's security risks, does present a formidable disposal problem, as we have seen.) It would be possible, although it hasn't been done, to run existing U.S. nuclear power plants on *mixed oxide fuel* (MOX)—diluted plutonium mixed with uranium—or to alter the plants to run on

At Hanford, plutonium nitrate solutions
were converted into plutonium metal
"buttons" the size of hockey pucks.

diluted plutonium alone. Neither diluted plutonium
nor MOX is, however, economically competitive with
plain uranium fuel.

Furthermore, converting nuclear power plants to
burn plutonium would require public hearings that the
nuclear power industry would much rather avoid. Finally, even if the economic and political pitfalls to using

plutonium power weren't enough to discourage a utility company, the dismal records of civilian reprocessing and breeder reactors in America would clinch the argument.

U.S. CIVILIAN REPROCESSING AND BREEDER REACTORS

From the beginning, the U.S. weapons program has reprocessed spent fuel to extract uranium and plutonium. In the early days of civilian nuclear power, utility companies too were attracted to the idea of reprocessing their spent fuel. This wouldn't have solved the high-level waste problem. On the contrary, reprocessing creates a greater volume of high-level wastes that, as at Hanford, not only contain most of the spent fuel's radioactivity but also are chemically contaminated. And reprocessing produces fresh fuel that itself ultimately re-enters the high-level waste stream.

Instead, the appeal of civilian reprocessing was twofold. It would provide uranium, which nuclear proponents used to fear would soon become scarce and expensive. (It hasn't. Mined uranium has instead become cheaper and more plentiful, and there's no shortage on the horizon.) Also, plutonium used as fuel could potentially supply virtually inexhaustible energy in *breeder reactors*—nuclear reactors designed to produce more plutonium than they burn.

Only two commercial reprocessing plants were ever built in the United States. Only one ever operated, at West Valley, New York. The West Valley plant operated between 1966 and 1972. Plagued by technical problems, it never came close to being profitable. Its high-level wastes remain on-site, awaiting vitrification and a multibillion-dollar cleanup.

In 1977, President Jimmy Carter put on hold any further development of civilian reprocessing in the United States. Civilian and military reprocessing use the same technology. Carter was concerned that encouraging civilian reprocessing would fuel the worldwide *proliferation* of the materials used to make nuclear weapons. Years later, President Ronald Reagan officially rescinded this policy, but civilian nuclear reprocessing was never revived in the United States. There just didn't seem to be any profit in it.

The U.S. breeder reactor program has met a similar, though much more contentious, fate. Breeder reactors pose much greater technological challenges than conventional nuclear reactors. Scientists struggled for years to overcome these technical hurdles, while policy makers and environmentalists argued about the breeder's potential merits and dangers. After a total of $8.74 billion had been spent over the years on research and development, the DOE's 1995 budget proposal killed the breeder program on the grounds that it was not economically competitive and that further development of the technology would only encourage the worldwide proliferation of nuclear weapons.[7]

NEW PLUTONIUM POLICIES

Concerns about proliferation have shaped America's changing policies on what to do with plutonium now that the Cold War arms race has ended. Early on, the

DOE viewed plutonium from decommissioned weapons as a "national asset" that it proposed to store, not bury as waste, at a long-term retrievable repository, perhaps at the Nevada Test Site.[8]

But America's national security might best be enhanced by giving up this "national asset," or at least relinquishing exclusive control over it. In 1994, after the United States agreed with Russia to allow each country to inspect the other's stored plutonium from dismantled weapons, a U.S. official called this agreement "the beginning of an international control regime over plutonium."[9]

Soon thereafter, in an effort to prod Russia and other nuclear nations into taking similar steps, the United States formally submitted part of its surplus plutonium and weapons-grade uranium to control by the International Atomic Energy Agency (IAEA), a United Nations organization. "We intend eventually," said a State Department spokesman, "to submit all fissile material no longer needed for the U.S. defense programs [to inspection] by the IAEA"[10]

Control of these weapons materials is a high-stakes game. In a September 1993 speech to the United Nations, President Bill Clinton noted that "growing stockpiles of plutonium and highly enriched uranium are raising the dangers of nuclear terrorism for all nations." He promised to work toward international agreement banning "production of these materials for weapons forever."[11]

The President stopped short, however, of advocating a flat, universal ban on *any* plutonium production. In a letter to members of Congress on this issue, Clinton explained:

> The United States does not encourage the
> civil use of plutonium. Its continued produc-
> tion is not justified on either economic or na-
> tional security grounds, and its accumulation
> creates serious proliferation and security dan-
> gers. I have not, however, called for a treaty
> banning all fissile material production. Such
> a proposal would breach existing U.S. com-
> mitments [and would] lead to confrontation
> with Russia and our allies.[12]

While the United States is neither reprocessing civilian
fuel nor pursuing breeder reactor technology, other nations—including some of the United States' most important allies and trading partners—are.

Nuclear issues, including the problems of nuclear
waste, pose formidable diplomatic problems for the
United States. The potential for ecological catastrophes
and for weapons proliferation gives Americans a strong
stake in how others handle nuclear technology and dispose of nuclear waste. The United States has been a
key participant in the international regulation of nuclear
technology. The international nuclear picture is a complicated one, however, and America's nuclear concerns
and priorities often conflict with even those of its allies.

CHAPTER SEVEN
INTERNATIONAL
ISSUES AND THE
NUCLEAR FUTURE

This book has been about nuclear waste in the United States. It would not be complete, however, without a quick examination of nuclear waste outside the U.S., for how other nations handle their wastes has a real impact on Americans.

WESTERN EUROPE
AND JAPAN

Western Europe, which has much smaller fossil fuel reserves than the United States does, has long relied on nuclear power as an important source of electricity. Although most West European plants are similar to U.S. models (indeed, American contractors helped to build many of them), nuclear power has developed differently across the Atlantic in several significant ways.

An experimental plutonium fuel breeder
reactor in Tsuruga City, Japan.

Unlike in the United States, reprocessing of spent fuel from civilian power reactors has been the intended norm in Europe. Not all nations with nuclear power reactors have reprocessing facilities, however. As of the mid-1990s, only Great Britain and, on a smaller scale, France were operating commercial reprocessing plants.[1] These facilities have contracted to reprocess spent fuel from many nations in Europe and beyond.

Another difference is that Europe's flirtation with breeder reactor technology has gone a lot further than America's. France started up a prototype breeder reactor only to have technical problems shut it down in 1988. In 1994 it returned to operation with the announced intention of being converted at some future date to a research reactor configured to burn more plutonium than it creates. Great Britain had planned to operate a controversial whole series of breeder reactors; that program too has sputtered to an end.

Japan, which has few domestic energy resources, has made a greater commitment to breeder reactor technology than any other nation. However, in 1994, shortly before its $5 billion prototype breeder reactor was due to start up, Japan announced that it was postponing much of its ambitious breeder program. This "postponement" was widely interpreted as an effective cancellation, and the Japanese breeder program is expected to grind slowly to a halt. Why? Technical problems and cost overruns have made it a financial fiasco, while problems with plutonium have generated international controversy.

Although Japan has pledged not to stockpile plutonium, delays in its breeder program have meant that tons of reprocessed plutonium intended for the program will have to be stored somewhere for years. Japan may end up burning much of the expensive stuff in conventional reactors just to get rid of it. Furthermore, since Japan's own reprocessing facilities aren't yet completed, the plutonium is being reprocessed in France and Great Britain. (Japan helped to finance these reprocessing plants, and Japanese contracts go a long way toward keeping the plants in business.) Thus, Japan's spent fuel, and then the reprocessed plutonium, must be shipped halfway around the world, creating a security problem and ecological risks that environmental groups have vehemently protested.

TRANSPORTATION AND PROLIFERATION HAZARDS

A ship belonging to the international environmental organization Greenpeace followed the first shipment of plutonium destined for Japan, which left France in November 1992. Two months and 17,000 miles (27,000 kilometers) later, more than one ton of plutonium reached its Japanese port. The freighter had long since outrun the slower Greenpeace craft, but not before Greenpeace had made the point that such shipments were inherently risky. A shipwreck could become an ecological catastrophe, and a ton of plutonium, enough to build dozens of nuclear weapons, offers a powerful temptation to piracy.

The more that nuclear wastes are shipped internationally (and Great Britain and France plan many such shipments, within Europe as well as beyond), the more

Greenpeace demonstrators pass in front
of the Japanese freighter, *Akatsuki Maru,*
as it is loaded with a container of plutonium
in Cherbourg, France.

opportunities there are for accidents or hijackings of nuclear materials. Opponents of reprocessing have pointed
out that there is no legitimate civilian need for plutonium (except, perhaps, in Japan's breeder program).
The world already has a glut of plutonium. Only risks
and no benefits, they say, are derived from continued
production.

Nonetheless, reprocessing plants keep producing more. A Rand Corporation study in November 1993 noted that civilian reprocessing programs were planning to produce more weapons-usable plutonium by the year 2003 than was scheduled to be freed up by the dismantling of nuclear weapons.[2] By 1993, Great Britain alone had accumulated 40 tons of plutonium for which it had no use—and it was about to start up a new reprocessing plant. Jessica Matthews, a senior fellow at the Council on Foreign Relations, suggested an unusual, though only partial, solution to ease the plutonium problem:

> [Great Britain's] foreign contracts require it to receive spent fuel and return plutonium and wastes. Britain can do both *without ever turning on the plant*. It can simply send back plutonium and wastes from its own supply. True, this puts plutonium into global commerce, but it has the great advantage of not adding a gram to the global supply.[3]

Plutonium glut notwithstanding, Great Britain did start up its new plant, THORP (Thermal Oxide Reprocessing Plant), at the Sellafield complex, early in 1994.

The reprocessing trade offers increasing opportunities for nuclear materials to be diverted to bomb production, but these aren't the only opportunities for diversion. Only a handful of the world's nations possess nuclear weapons. Thirty-odd nations, however, use nuclear power. Some of these nations are ambitious to join the nuclear weapons club. In 1974, India joined the nuclear club by exploding a nuclear device powered by plutonium derived, in an Indian reprocessing plant, from spent fuel from its nuclear power production.

Since then, nations that use nuclear power have submitted to an international inspection system intended to ensure that spent fuel and other nuclear materials aren't diverted to weapons production. The system has not been completely successful: The nuclear club has grown, and nuclear-ambitious nations such as North Korea have balked at full compliance with the inspection regimen.

THE FORMER SOVIET UNION

Russia possesses the world's largest stockpile of plutonium, an estimated 180 tons of it.[4] As Russia meets its treaty obligations by decommissioning thousands of the former Soviet Union's nuclear weapons, concern has grown both in Russia and in the West about the possibility of nuclear materials going astray. Russia's flourishing organized crime syndicates have reportedly filched bomb materials for black-market sales. The Russian government itself, desperate for cash, has sought more legitimate, though still risky, ways to profit from its nuclear stockpiles.

The United States has a strong interest in minimizing these risks. To this end, the U.S. Enrichment Corporation (a spinoff from the Department of Energy) has agreed to buy up billions of dollars' worth of HEU (highly enriched uranium) from dismantled Russian and Ukranian warheads; the uranium will be diluted to fuel power plants.[5] Plutonium is a knottier problem. On the one hand, a U.S. firm has been exploring the possibility of contracting with Russia to build a power plant to burn it; on the other hand, various observers have urged that the United States or a consortium of Western nations should buy up Russia's plutonium to ensure its safekeeping. The policy of the United States on this issue is not yet set.

Nor is it yet clear how extensively the United States and other Western nations would be involved in cleaning up the former Soviet bloc's various nuclear messes. The Soviet Union's nuclear weapons facilities are concentrated in ten closed "nuclear cities," each of which has generated far greater health and environmental hazards than even the worst U.S. weapons sites. For example, near Chelyabinsk, in the Ural Mountains, a 1957 explosion released perhaps 2 million curies of radiation over a wide area. Russian officials have acknowledged that radioactive wastes equivalent to "twenty Chernobyls" remain at the site of the Chelyabinsk disaster.[6]

Western attention has focused less, however, on the military complexes than on the former Soviet Union's nuclear power plants, in fear that the 1986 Chernobyl disaster—the worst nuclear power plant accident ever—might repeat itself. In 1993 more than 10 percent of Ukraine's national budget was earmarked for cleaning up after Chernobyl.[7] The cleanup effort has been so slipshod and underfunded that fires have periodically broken out at the facility and the concrete shell built to contain the burned-out reactor has crumbled and threatens to collapse. Furthermore, lax security at the site has raised fears that nuclear materials might be stolen from it. Nonetheless, in 1992, Ukraine, desperate for energy and unable to pay for it abroad, restarted two undamaged reactors at the Chernobyl complex. In the following year its parliament voted to keep them running indefinitely.

The Chernobyl plant is by no means unique. In 1993, of the 57 nuclear power plants operating in the nations of the former Soviet Union, experts believed that 25 were "very dangerous," including 15 built with a Chernobyl-type design.[8] Still more dangerous plants built with Soviet technology operate in various East European countries. The nations saddled with these plants can afford neither to shut them all down nor to modify them to make them safer.

Western nations have agreed to help pay for cleaning up Soviet nuclear sites and for improving the safety of Soviet-bloc nuclear power plants. (Much of the money is expected to go to Western contractors.) But arguments over exactly how the money should be allocated, together with Russia's reluctance to allow unrestricted access to its facilities, have hampered the effort. By 1994, little money had actually been spent.

UNDERGROUND INJECTION AND OCEAN DUMPING

The health, safety, and environmental sins of the Soviet Union's nuclear technology extend to its nuclear waste disposal. Many of Russia's cleanup problems are far worse than anything the DOE has to contend with, and Russia has made far less progress than the DOE in finding solutions for its problems.

Earlier Soviet efforts to dispose of nuclear waste created a new set of hazards. Beginning in the early

1960s, low-level and high-level nuclear wastes were pumped directly (with no protective containers) into the earth at three separate sites in Russia: Tomsk, Krasnoyarsk, and Dimitrovgrad. The wells into which these unshielded wastes were injected were only 650 to 4,600 feet (200 to 1,400 meters) deep—much shallower than the several-miles-deep nuclear burial option considered by some Western nations. Russian scientists in 1994 acknowledged that "about half of all the radioactive materials produced in Russia" had been injected at these sites, each of which is located near a major river. In 1995 scientists were still evaluating where the nuclear wastes were located, how they might move underground, and what dangers they might pose to the environment and to human health.[9]

In addition to what was injected into the earth, nuclear wastes have been dumped indiscriminately within the former Soviet Union and extensively, over many years, in the world's oceans. Not only the former Soviet Union but also various Western nations have dumped nuclear wastes in the oceans. Until 1970 the United States was among them. In 1972, however, the London Convention banned all ocean dumping of high-level nuclear wastes. And in 1983 a temporary moratorium on the dumping of even low-level wastes was declared. (Several nuclear nations that wished to keep their options open abstained when this ban was made permanent in 1993.)

Also in 1993, after years of denial, Russia admitted that it had for many years scuttled decommissioned nuclear submarines as well as dumped tens of thousands of containers of high-level and low-level nuclear waste, mostly in Arctic waters. Russian spokesmen indicated

A variety of waste that must be sorted
and either disposed of or stored.

that they did not wish to continue ocean dumping, but
that with few other options they might be forced to do
so. Dozens of aging nuclear subs were scheduled for
decommissioning, and nuclear wastes with no place else
to go were piling up in storage on rusting retired ships
anchored in Russian waters.

Nuclear power is widespread and well established. In 1992, 417 nuclear power reactors were running in 31 nations, producing 17 percent of the world's electricity.[10] Although the trend in the United States and in some West European nations has been not to build new plants, other nations have planned expansive nuclear programs. Developing nations, China in particular, nurture hopes that nuclear power will fuel their economic growth.

Whether or not this next great wave of nuclear power actually materializes, nuclear power—and nuclear waste—will be with us for many years to come. The waste stream even from Western nations will grow, not dwindle, in the years ahead as refueling continues and plants are decommissioned. Most of the waste will be low-level, and most of it will likely be buried, although more people are becoming wary of the hazards of such burial. As for the high-level waste, except for Russia's dumping, no permanent disposal of high-level waste has yet taken place in any country. What its ultimate fate will be is anyone's guess.

NOTES

CHAPTER ONE
THE BOMB AND NUCLEAR BASICS

1. Gerard H. Clarfield and William M. Wiecek, *Nuclear America: Military and Civilian Nuclear Power in the United States, 1940–1980* (New York: Harper & Row, 1984), p. 51.
2. Nicholas Lenssen, *Nuclear Waste: The Problem That Won't Go Away*, Worldwatch Paper #106 (Washington, D.C.: Worldwatch Institute, 1991), p. 20.
3. *Washington Post*, December 8, 1993.
4. Lenssen, p. 13.
5. League of Women Voters, *Nuclear Waste Primer* (New York: Lyons and Burford, 1993), p. 124.
6. *Nuclear Waste Primer*, p. 125.
7. Ibid., pp. 125–126.

CHAPTER TWO
NUCLEAR POWER IN THE
UNITED STATES

1. Gerard H. Clarfield and William M. Wiecek, *Nuclear America: Military and Civilian Nuclear Power in the United States, 1940–1980* (New York: Harper & Row, 1984), p. 200.

2. Ibid., p. 280.
3. Congressional Research Service data cited in March 1992 Safe Energy Communication Council news release.
4. Author's telephone interview with Chris Nichols at SECC, June 2, 1994.
5. Nicholas Lenssen, *Nuclear Waste: The Problem That Won't Go Away*, Worldwatch Paper #106 (Washington, D.C.: Worldwatch Institute, 1991), p. 36.
6. League of Women Voters, *Nuclear Waste Primer* (New York: Lyons and Burford, 1993), pp. 67–68.
7. *Washington Post*, February 5, 1993.
8. *New York Times*, August 27, 1993.

CHAPTER THREE
CLEANING UP AFTER
NUCLEAR POWER

1. League of Women Voters, *Nuclear Waste Primer* (New York: Lyons and Burford, 1993), p. 73.
2. *New York Times*, December 10, 1992.
3. Ibid., May 21 and August 23, 1993.
4. *Washington Post*, November 26, 1993.
5. Steve Romano of U.S. Ecology, quoted in *New York Times*, January 24, 1994.
6. Department of Energy figures cited by several sources.
7. *New York Times*, December 28, 1992, and *Nuclear Waste Primer*, p. 81.
8. Nicholas Lenssen, *Nuclear Waste: The Problem That Won't Go Away*, Worldwatch Paper #106 (Washington, D.C.: Worldwatch Institute, 1991), p. 9.
9. *New York Times*, December 3, 1993.
10. *Nuclear Waste Primer*, p. 40.
11. Lenssen, pp. 34, 45.
12. Tom Cotton, formerly with the United States Office of Technology Assessment, quoted in *Boston Globe*, May 17, 1993.
13. *New York Times*, December 8, 1992.
14. Ibid., March 28, 1994.

15. U.S. House of Representatives, Committee on Natural Resources, Subcommittee on Oversight and Investigations, Majority Staff Report, *Deep Pockets: Taxpayer Liability for Environmental Contamination*, July 1993, p. 23. The report suggests that the DOE should keep a close eye on the millage rate, adjusting it to try to compensate for early closings.
16. "MacNeil/Lehrer NewsHour," PBS telecast, January 13, 1994.
17. Kai Erikson, "Out of Sight, Out of Our Minds," *New York Times Magazine*, March 6, 1994. This article was adapted from Erikson's book *A New Species of Trouble* (New York: Norton, 1994).
18. Lenssen, pp. 36–37.
19. Ibid., p. 37.
20. *Boston Globe*, May 17, 1993.
21. *Washington Post*, December 9, 1992.
22. "MacNeil/Lehrer NewsHour," PBS telecast, January 13, 1994.
23. *Nuclear Waste Primer*, p. 52.
24. Erikson, "Out of Sight, Out of Our Minds."
25. "MacNeil/Lehrer NewsHour," PBS telecast, January 13, 1994.
26. *Washington Post*, March 3, 1993.
27. *New York Times*, December 3, 1994.
28. "MacNeil/Lehrer NewsHour," PBS telecast, January 13, 1994.
29. Jeffrey Davis, "Bikini's Silver Lining," *New York Times Magazine*, May 1, 1994.
30. *New York Times*, August 8, 1993.
31. Ibid., August 27, 1993.
32. Luther J. Carter, *Washington Post* opinion page, August 22, 1993.
33. *Nuclear Waste Primer*, p. 44.
34. Scott Saleska, staff scientist at the Institute for Energy and Environmental Research, quoted in Lenssen, p. 23.
35. All Erikson quotes are from "Out of Sight, Out of Our Minds."

CHAPTER FOUR
NUCLEAR WEAPONS PRODUCTION

1. C. P. Snow, on secrecy in science, quoted in Michael D'Antonio, *Atomic Harvest: Hanford and the Lethal Toll of America's Nuclear Arsenal* (New York: Crown, 1993), p. 206.
2. Per 1990 interview with Wayne Hansen, "the Los Alamos scientist in charge of environmental compliance," Tad Bartimus and Scott McCartney, *Trinity's Children: Living Along America's Nuclear Highway* (New York: Harcourt Brace Jovanovich, 1991), p. 119.
3. Bartimus and McCartney, pp. 188–192.
4. D'Antonio, pp. 251, 257.
5. Bartimus and McCartney, pp. 193–194.
6. *New York Times*, December 5, 1992.
7. Grand jury report quoted in *Washington Post*, November 22, 1992.
8. League of Women Voters, *Nuclear Waste Primer* (New York: Lyons and Burford, 1993), p. 96.
9. D'Antonio, p. 287.
10. Ibid., p. 220.
11. Ibid., p. 241.
12. Ibid., p. 270.
13. Ibid.
14. *New York Times*, January 4, 1994.
15. Ibid., May 6, 1993.
16. *Washington Post*, March 31, 1994.

CHAPTER FIVE
CLEANING UP AFTER THE ARMS RACE

1. Michael D'Antonio, *Atomic Harvest: Hanford and the Lethal Toll of America's Nuclear Arsenal* (New York: Crown, 1993), p. 263.
2. Office of Technology Assessment, *Complex Cleanup: The Environmental Legacy of Nuclear Weapons Production* (Washington, D.C.: Government Printing Office, 1991).

3. League of Women Voters, *Nuclear Waste Primer* (New York: Lyons and Burford, 1993), p. 123.
4. *Washington Post*, December 19, 1993.
5. *Nuclear Waste Primer*, pp. 122–123.
6. Ibid., p. 118.
7. *New York Times*, October 22, 1993.
8. Ibid.
9. Ibid., June 30, 1993, and *Washington Post*, August 10, 1993, and January 9, 1994.
10. *New York Times*, December 8, 1993.
11. Ibid., June 21, 1993.
12. All figures in this paragraph are from *Nuclear Waste Primer*, pp. 108–109.
13. D'Antonio, pp. 98, 285.
14. *Washington Post*, May 15, 1993.
15. *New York Times*, June 21, 1993.
16. Ibid., December 24, 1992.
17. Ibid., July 11, 1993.
18. Ibid., August 15, 1993.
19. Ibid., December 10, 1993.
20. Ibid., April 4, 1993.
21. Ibid., June 21 and October 3, 1993.
22. Ibid., June 21, 1993.
23. *Washington Post*, February 17, 1993.
24. Ibid., November 21, 1992.
25. Ibid., November 30, 1993.

CHAPTER SIX
THE PROBLEM OF PLUTONIUM

1. Lester R. Brown et al., *State of the World 1994* (New York: Norton, 1994), p. 142.
2. Department of Energy announcement reported in *Washington Post*, December 8, 1993. According to *New York Times*, May 20, 1994, the department subsequently acknowledged that somewhat more plutonium than this has actually accumulated over the years; it's not clear exactly how much.
3. Office of Technology Assessment estimates cited in *New York Times*, October 31, 1993.

4. *New York Times*, October 31, 1993.
5. Ibid., June 1, 1994.
6. *Washington Post*, January 23, 1994.
7. Ibid., February 12, 1994.
8. *Federal Register*, July 23, 1993. DOE notice. Cited in *Washington Post*, July 28, 1993.
9. *Washington Post*, March 16, 1994.
10. *New York Times*, March 24, 1994.
11. *Washington Post*, October 1, 1993.
12. Ibid., November 12, 1993.

CHAPTER SEVEN
INTERNATIONAL ISSUES AND
THE NUCLEAR FUTURE

1. Greenpeace press release, London, June 1, 1993.
2. *Washington Post*, November 13, 1993.
3. *Washington Post* opinion page, November 28, 1993.
4. *Washington Post*, April 8, 1993.
5. *New York Times*, January 18, 1994.
6. *Washington Post*, January 28, 1993.
7. Ibid., October 22, 1993.
8. *New York Times*, April 8, 1993.
9. Ibid., November 21, 1994.
10. League of Women Voters, *Nuclear Waste Primer* (New York: Lyons and Burford, 1993), p. 61.

GLOSSARY

alpha radiation: the type of radiation that can do most damage to living tissue it touches, but that is least penetrating; it can't pass through skin but can cause cancer if particles emitting it are inhaled or swallowed; it is emitted by many radioisotopes with very long half-lives

arms race: a competition between nations to produce more or more-powerful weapons, as between the United States and the Soviet Union during the Cold War

beta radiation: a type of radiation that has more penetrating power than alpha radiation, but less than gamma radiation; found in most nuclear wastes; emitted by many radioisotopes with short half-lives

breeder reactor: a nuclear reactor configured to create more plutonium than it burns

chain reaction: the process by which an adequately fueled nuclear reaction sustains itself; one atom splits, releasing subatomic particles called neutrons, which induce additional atoms to split

downwinders: people living in the path of radioactive particles blown on the wind from nuclear weapons testing or production sites

enrichment: the process of concentrating uranium or plutonium to make fuel for nuclear reactors or, at much higher concentration, fuel for nuclear weapons

fallout: radioactive particles falling from the sky, mostly from aboveground testing of nuclear weapons

fission: a nuclear reaction in which atoms are split, releasing large amounts of energy

fusion: a nuclear reaction in which smaller atoms fuse into larger atoms, releasing far more energy than during a fission reaction

gamma radiation: a type of radiation that has more penetrating power than either alpha radiation or beta radiation; found in most nuclear wastes; emitted by many radioisotopes with short half-lives

half-life: the length of time it takes for half of the radioactivity in a particular material to decay

high-level waste: spent fuel from civilian or military nuclear reactors

highly enriched uranium (HEU): uranium that is sufficiently concentrated to be used for nuclear weapons

low-level waste: waste other than spent fuel that is contaminated with radioisotopes; typically much less intensely radioactive than high-level waste

meltdown: destruction of a nuclear reactor's core (where the fuel is) caused by an out-of-control nuclear reaction

military-industrial complex: a powerful, mutually supportive alliance of military bureaucracy, civilian defense contractors, and university research programs

mixed-oxide fuel (MOX): nuclear fuel that combines uranium and plutonium

nuclear reactor: a device in which a nuclear chain reaction is carefully begun, then sustained and controlled to allow harvesting of the reaction's energy or to produce plutonium, or both

nuclear weapon: a powerful weapon, far more destructive than conventional bombs, fueled by an explosively fast nuclear reaction *plutonium:* a radioactive element slightly heavier than uranium that occurs only in small quantities in nature, is created in nuclear reactors, and is used to fuel nuclear weapons

proliferation: increase in the number of nuclear weapons worldwide, and especially in the number of countries that possess them

radioactivity: the spontaneous emission of energetic particles by certain elements, such as uranium

radioisotopes: radioactive isotopes (isotopes are slightly different types of atoms of the same chemical element; they possess the same atomic number but have slightly different physical properties)

radionuclides: radioactive nuclides (nuclides are types of atoms of the same chemical element that possess exactly the same sort of nucleus)

radon gas: a colorless, odorless gas naturally emitted by radioactive elements in the earth

reprocessing: chemically treating spent nuclear reactor fuel to separate plutonium from the rest of it

strontium 90: a radioactive isotope of the element strontium that is found in radioactive fallout and that causes damage to people who ingest it

thermonuclear weapon: a hydrogen bomb, fueled by a fusion reaction among hydrogen atoms at very high temperatures generated by a nuclear fission reaction

transuranic: heavier than uranium; radioactive transuranic elements such as plutonium are mostly produced in nuclear reactors

uranium: a naturally occurring radioactive element, some isotopes of which are useful for fueling nuclear reactors and nuclear weapons

vitrification: the process of mixing with or turning something into glass; proposed as a way to encase high-level nuclear wastes and prevent them from ever contaminating water supplies

yellowcake: a crude, yellow uranium oxide derived from processing raw uranium ore

FOR FURTHER
INFORMATION

Barlett, Donald L., and James B. Steele. *Forevermore: Nuclear Waste in America*. New York: Norton, 1985.

Bartimus, Tad, and Scott McCartney. *Trinity's Children: Living Along America's Nuclear Highway*. New York: Harcourt Brace Jovanovich, 1991.

Clarfield, Gerard H., and William M. Wiecek. *Nuclear America: Military and Civilian Nuclear Power in the United States, 1940–1980*. New York: Harper & Row, 1984.

D'Antonio, Michael. *Atomic Harvest: Hanford and the Lethal Toll of America's Nuclear Arsenal*. New York: Crown Publishing Group, 1993.

League of Women Voters. *The Nuclear Waste Primer: A Handbook for Citizens*. New York: Lyons and Burford, 1993.

Lenssen, Nicholas. *Nuclear Waste: The Problem That Won't Go Away*. Worldwatch Paper #106. Washington, D.C.: Worldwatch Institute, 1991.

INDEX

Page numbers in *italics* refer to illustrations.

Environmental Protection Agency
(EPA), 23, 55, 66, 92
Erikson, Kai, 62-63

Fallout, 12, 14
Federal Facilities Compliance Act
(FFCA) of 1992, 77
Fission reaction, 15
France, 106, 107
Fuel rods, 21, 35, 47, 48
Fusion reaction, 15

Gamma radiation, 17-19, 22
Grand Junction, Colorado, 20
Great Britain, 14, 106, 107, 109
Greenpeace, 107, 108
Green Run, 73

Half-life, 17
Hanford Reservation, Washington,
69-70, 73-74, 77, 81, 86, 87, 89-
93, 100
Hazardous Materials Transportation
Uniform Safety Act of 1990, 26
High-level nuclear waste, 22-24, 26,
35, 45-47, 49-51, 53-58, 60-63,
70
Highly enriched uranium (HEU),
21, 94, 102, 110
Hiroshima, 11
Hydrogen bomb (H-bomb), 11,
15

Idaho National Engineering Lab
(INEL), 81, 83, 86, 87
India, 109
Indian Point, 25
Insurance, 28-29
International Atomic Energy Agency
(IAEA), 102
International Physicians for the Pre-
vention of Nuclear War, 14

Japan, 106-108
Justice Department, 68-69

Landfills, 22, 40, 42
Legal Environmental Assistance
Foundation, 76
London Convention, 113
Los Alamos, 64, 81, 83
Loss leader, 29, 31
Low-level nuclear waste, 22, 23, 39-
40, 41, 42, 44-45, 80-81
Low-Level Radioactive Waste Policy
Act of 1980, 40, 42, 44-45
Lyons, Kansas, 46

Manhattan Project, 11, 12, 64
Meltdown, 31-32
Military-industrial complex, 12
Milling and mining, 19-21, 20
Mississippi River, 50
Mixed oxide fuel (MOX), 98-99
Mixed-waste disposal, 23, 82-83

Nagasaki, 11
National Environmental Policy Act
(NEPA) of 1969, 76
Native Americans, 53, 60
Natural Resources Defense Council,
76
Neutrons, 15, 35
Nevada Test Site, 53, 54, 66, 80-
81, 102
North Korea, 110
Nuclear Regulatory Commission
(NRC), 23, 31, 34, 37, 49, 55
Nuclear Waste Fund, 46-47, 50
Nuclear Waste Policy Act of 1982,
46

Oak Ridge, 81, 83
Ocean dumping, 39, 113-114
O'Leary, Hazel, 56, 77, 78